HEALING

For Janie, my
Wellesley roommate,

with much love,

Jamae van Eck

HEALING

"Wilt Thou Be Made Whole?"

A Spiritual Answer

by

Jamae van Eck

Panthaleon Press

Printed in the United States of America. For information contact: **Panthaleon Press, P.O. Box 70669, Pasadena, California, 91117-7669, or call (800) 417-5220**

First Edition: 1997

Library of Congress Catalog Card Number: 96-92538

International Standard Book Number: 0-9653879-0-9

Includes bibliographical references and index.

Suggested classifications:
      1. Healing, Spiritual 2. Self-Help
      (Recovery from victimization) 3. Religion

Panthaleon (Pronounced păn tal´ ē ŏn. From the Greek, meaning "in all things conquerors or victors.")

"...in all these things we are more than conquerors through him that loved us."
(Rom. 8:37)

"Self-rejection is the greatest enemy of the spiritual life because it contradicts the sacred voice that calls us the 'Beloved.' Being the Beloved expresses the core truth of our existence... We are intimately loved long before our parents, teachers, spouses, children and friends loved or wounded us...

"Listening to that voice with great inner attentiveness, I hear at my center words that say: 'I have called you by name, from the very beginning. You are mine and I am yours...on you my favor rests. I have molded you in the depths of the earth and knitted you together in your mother's womb. I have carved you in the palms of my hands and hidden you in the shadow of my embrace...You belong to me. I am your father, your mother, your brother, your sister, your lover and your spouse...yes, even your child... wherever you are I will be. Nothing will ever separate us. We are one."

Henri Nouwen, Life of the Beloved, pp. 28-31

TABLE OF CONTENTS

PREFACE

When an eminent Harvard cardiologist and a legendary global investor collaborate in convening a three day conference of health professionals to explore the relationship between spirituality and healing, then an obvious and significant shift in attitudes and outlook in the United States with regard to healing is taking place. Just such an event, of striking importance and co-sponsored by Dr. Herbert Benson and Sir John Templeton, was held in Boston in December, 1995 with nearly one thousand attendees. Such interest in and acknowledgement of healing resulting from spirituality is both serious and expanding.

There are many other indicators of a fundamental change in attitudes: 1) the fact that roughly one-third of all Americans make use of "alternative" methods of healing, as reported in the New England Journal of Medicine in January, 1993. 2) A growing recognition of the "mind-body connection"—of the interrelationships between thought, feeling, emotion, and bodily health. 3) The increasing involvement of main line churches in healing ministries, from regular healing services in many Methodist churches, to the Order of St. Luke in the Episcopal Church, to the Stephen Ministry in U.C.C. congregations, to the charismatic movement in Catholic and other faiths, to consistent healing "signs" in Pentecostal services. 4) The spectacular recent rise in both offerings and sales of what are denominated "inspirational" books, including those that focus on self-help and healing.

Add to these indicators a growing criticism of traditional medical approaches and conventional medical wisdom and their horrendous costs brought recently to the surface by the great national health-care debate. Add also the acknowledgment by many natural scientists, particularly quantum physicists, that reality is fundamentally "observer-

xiii

created," and the shift in perspectives is plain. One may well wonder whether, at the onset of the third millennium, thinking on the subject of human health or wholeness is not coming full circle. Could it be, after all, that the teaching and practice of a humble but uniquely endowed Galilean named Jesus holds the key to mankind's salvation—to healing?

Are we at the point of realizing that invention and technology have had their day? Do we finally understand that gains in material well-being, if devoid of spiritual meaning and moral value, are ultimately self-defeating? Time will tell. But my own conclusion, based on more than a half-century of proving and three decades of professional practice, is that the needed answers as well as the fundamental means for healing both individual and social woes are inherently spiritual, and that humanity as a whole is on the threshold of awakening to this fact.

This book provides insights into this conclusion. It offers a perspective on healing that is at once spiritual and scientific—that is, repeatable, verifiable, demonstrable. Its incubus was a thesis completed at Boston University's School of Theology for a Master's Degree in Theological Studies, but its heart lies in individual stories of healing, including my own.

The book deals especially with recovery from victimization: not only the experience of being a victim—being wounded, hurt, betrayed, damaged, harmed—and its consequences, when one is labelled a victim and so treated by others, but also when one assumes the role of victim and literally becomes his own worst enemy. Its message relates to the hope and possibility that survivors can not only triumph spiritually over the multiple consequences of what they have suffered but can themselves become "wounded healers"—able to assist others.

The book will draw on other publications, not only the writings of those who have explored recently and in depth the effects of trauma, but those who are actively engaged with healing that is inner and spiritual, hence transformative, in both essence and outcome. Most authors concur in the recognition that secrecy or hiddenness is the greatest single deterrent to confronting and resolving both the internal injuries and external behaviors arising out of whatever causes harm. The imperative is always to "know thyself" whenever the need for healing, renewal, redemption arises.

I also note in the book voices to be heeded warning of the dangers in fostering a "victim mentality"—of some who would personally profit from the sufferings of others, and of the enormous damage that results when those who suffer are encouraged to habitually accuse or blame others for their own often self-induced difficulties. The growing recognition among professionals and their patients of the inseparability of thought (one's belief-systems, attitudes, feelings) and body in the process of healing will be considered as well. At issue is the fundamental question of how best to break the bonds of hopelessness, despair, and incurability that hinder recovery.

Society in general has erred substantially on the side of ignoring, neglecting, excusing, or concealing violence and inhumanity, especially when that inhumanity is directed at the marginalized and dependent—at children, at the poor, the aged, or at women who are usually less able to fend for themselves. Moreover, so long as economic structures, cultural mores, or theological doctrines place some members of society in a subordinate and defenseless position, such inhumanity is likely to continue.

People can be victims in many ways—of circumstances of birth and nationality, of natural disasters, of lack of vocational or educational opportunity, of accident and disease, of crime, abuse, or war. Webster's definition of victim as "...a person subjected to oppression, deprivation, or suffering; someone who suffers death, loss, or injury...; someone tricked, duped, or subjected to hardship; someone badly used or taken advantage of..." (Third New International Dictionary) expands the scope of the term.

A major contention of this book is that it is not so much the circumstances or the presenting cause of trauma as one's own view of it or reaction to it that gives any tragedy or offense power to harm or disable—that is, to continue to make a victim of the individual.

Such reaction is particularly devastating when the abuse is sexual and is directed at children—an area to which the book gives particular attention. Recent studies have shown the long-term negative effect of early sexual trauma, not only on one's self-image, but on the child's entire recognition of, and ability to appeal to, a redemptive, divine power or influence. Still, the promise in Isaiah (45:5), "I girded thee, though thou hast not known me," can be seen to be fulfilled in individual lives. This inner voice, if heeded, can keep one from his or her own undoing.

The focus of the Biblically-based method of recovery presented in this book is on individual transformation and redemption—on heeding the inner voice that heals. Still, society in general can't be excused from making wise, informed, and effective efforts to mitigate the effects of tragedies beyond an individual's control, and to both stem and reform attitudes and practices that foster victimization.

Some systems theorists point out that whatever alters a system (a family, organizational, community, or national system) will affect all individuals within that system. But conversely, whatever changes one individual within a system will affect the entire system. It is my experience that real and lasting change proceeds from the inward to the outward and from the individual to society as a whole. In the book, I draw on that experience, encompassing thirty years of encouraging healing for individuals struggling with a wide range of victimizing problems.

The book will also build bridges of understanding and establish commonalities of purpose and approach with those in the helping professions: medical, psychiatric, ministerial, social, and educational. All such professionals are concerned with change that betters, comforts, and heals, with enabling individuals to cope with, understand, and eventually transcend the sometimes paralyzing, crippling difficulties they encounter.

Nevertheless, I write, not so much for the professional, as for the lay reader. Through the book, I provide fresh insights and fundamentally spiritual answers for those struggling with behaviors that are inherently abnormal and self-destructive, with relationship difficulties, with the sometimes crippling fears that both precede and accompany the onset of disease, and with the pervasive poor self-esteem that so often engenders chronic ills. It goes without saying that the purpose of this book about healing is healing.

A poor or mistaken self-definition, arising out of a sense of alienation from God and a consequent feeling of spiritual meaninglessness or void, is at the root of most mental and physical disorders, whereas even some glimpse of one's spiritual selfhood as a child of God heals.

As with many others who write, my interest in this subject is more than purely academic or professional. It is also personal. From a family of origin that was "dysfunctional" in terms of physical and emotional abuse, to a situation where my own children, without my knowledge, suffered periodic abuse within the home at the hands of older children of trusted family friends and neighbors employed as baby-sitters, I have travelled the same road or made the same journey others must also make.

I know it isn't an easy road. I also know it's often more possible to cope with, to reform and even forgive violence directed at one's self than to be free of anguish, remorse, anger, and guilt over the desecration of what you most dearly love. Early sexual abuse is possibly the most crippling trauma a child can endure. Humanly, it can be determinative of the child's whole sense of identity, including his boundaries and relationships with others. Undiscovered and untreated, it tends to perpetuate failure and hopelessness for years to come. Leonard Shengold (1989) refers to it as "soul-murder."

I take exception to his term. My contention is that the "soul"—the true selfhood of the individual—is inherently spiritual and God-determined, hence indestructible. This spiritual selfhood is the ultimate reality of each of us, and the human personality so hurtfully impacted by trauma and discord is its mask or counterfeit.

Despite much outward evidence to the contrary, my perspective, aided by the stories and victories of many others, is that no one is beyond hope, no circumstance beyond redemption, no entrenched attitudes or behaviors beyond correcting, no anguish beyond healing. Everyone ultimately has a choice between remaining a victim or rising beyond that demoralizing self-concept. My purpose is to foster a healthy, positive choice—a choice that has power to put an end to the often intergenerational effects of violence and abusiveness and to transform and heal.

In this effort, I must express gratitude to numerous spiritual guides over many years, to the authors and teachers who have opened important windows of understanding to me, to my children who have been patient and forgiving of me, to many students and clients of my own who have learned with me and whose healings have nurtured my own, and to my husband of two and a half years who has supported this effort and who has unfolded to me more than I have ever before known of the real meaning of love.

I am a child of the church. Hence, my entire faith is Biblically grounded. I have also been, since my teens, a practitioner of scientific Christianity. That is, I have endeavored to live in accord with and put into practice the immutable laws of God and to discern the spiritual reality that transcends human circumstances and has power to transform them. This book shares my understanding of this reality. It illustrates spirituality that is essential and practical, religion that is not palliative and superficial but remedial and central.

Prayer is not a retreat from reality but an awakening to it, and health is not a state of body or matter, but of mind, soul and spirit. I dedicate this book to all who seek Truth and who, to the best of their ability, live it through Love—who endeavor to be that temple of God which is holy in which the Spirit of God dwells (I Cor.3:16-17), and which, finally, is beyond and above desecration.

Jamae van Eck

San Marino, California
December, 1996

Chapter One

IMPORTANT QUESTIONS

*"Be ye transformed by the renewing
of your mind" (Rom. 12:2)*

In the fifth chapter of John's Gospel there is an account of Jesus' healing of a man "which had an infirmity thirty and eight years." Many sick and afflicted people remained at the pool of Bethesda, "waiting for the moving of the water," hoping for some miraculous divine intervention to heal them.

Jesus asks the man a curious question: "Do you want to be healed?" ("Wilt thou be made whole?" in the King James Version).

The man doesn't say Yes, but instead explains that he has no one to put him into the pool; others get there ahead of him. Jesus then commands the man to "Rise, take up thy bed and walk."

In their brief conversation, Jesus challenges the man. Apparently without knowledge of the circumstances, and without making any lengthy analysis or examination of the man's physical or mental state, Jesus simply commands him to rise. With the authority of the Christ, of spiritual reality and divine Truth, Jesus demands the man rise up out of that crippling sense of passivity, that he "take up his bed" and with it the entrenched sense of powerlessness and lack of worth in which he had lain for so long, and walk.

The man responds and is immediately healed.

Jesus was insisting that the man make a choice, a decision, to change not others, not society, not any

1

circumstances, but only his own thinking or outlook and so progress. There really was no more appropriate or compassionate thing Jesus could have done; no more spiritually effective way the man's needs could have been met. Afterward, Jesus finds him in the temple and tells him to "sin no more"—never again to believe in or accept a power greater than God—"lest a worse thing come unto thee."

What Jesus brought to the man at the pool of Bethesda was a totally different perspective—a glimpse of an alternative or ultimate reality powerful enough to transform the man's entire sense of himself as a pitiable, hopeless mortal. The man then rose to a higher concept—he was, in religious terminology, re-born, renewed, regenerated, redeemed—and he subsequently took responsibility for his own thoughts and behavior.

Had the man reached a point of readiness to respond to such spiritual insight? Apparently. Was he willing to stop relying on others, or even on efforts to change the outward circumstances, and instead change his own way of thinking? So it seems. Was there anything that might have been done to hasten this readiness and either mitigate or lessen his long years of suffering? Certainly.

There were great multitudes of sick people at Bethesda, and, so far as we know, Jesus healed just this one. Some argue that this story has no relevance at all for us today; that Jesus' healing ability was divinely derived and delegated just to him, a dispensation never to be repeated. Yet, from the Gospels, it's plain that Jesus instructed his followers to heal, and they did. Moreover, Jesus set the example, he marked the way to a practical, redemptive Christianity, and if we would do the works he did, we must follow.

There can be drawn from this incident significant lessons for all who, like the man waiting at the pool, feel themselves victims of circumstances. Clearly the man was struggling with a sense of resignation and hopelessness, of self-pity and despair.

Today, in Western culture with its rising social consciousness and extensive social programs, the man would, in all likelihood, be entrenched in his disability by well-meaning but often ineffective efforts to deal with his problems from exclusively physical or environmental standpoints, but with little or inadequate reference to his own point of view.

In that era, because of his affliction, the man would have been excluded from worship, regarded as inherently bad or sinful and worthy of punishment. In either case, his difficulties would only be augmented not alleviated by others, and the underlying "sin" or mistaken and self-defeating mind-set would not be corrected.

Why does someone, for decades, remain hopelessly crippled or impotent, stuck in a posture or problem that doesn't yield? Why aren't suffering individuals healed or at least helped?

It is essential for us to address these questions in light of the enormous problems in both health care and welfare reform with which governmental bodies and private agencies alike are now struggling. Reform is impelled not only by the threat, both to individuals and society, of ruinous financial costs but also by the fact that present systems aren't accomplishing their goals and are even generating collateral problems of their own.

Change is also driven by an exploding awareness of the extent of victimization in our culture and the mounting consequences, both to individuals and to society as a whole, arising from it.

A <u>Wall Street Journal</u> editorial entitled "White Fright," for example, pointed to the skyrocketing illegitimacy rate—up 54% overall since 1980 in the United States, and its connection to violence, abuse (both sexual and substance), and to crime, poverty, illiteracy, disease, and homelessness (19 June, 1995).

Isn't it possible that such problems are worsening, despite the best-intentioned public and private programs established to deal with them, because the basic belief-systems underlying the problems aren't addressed? Moreover, individual responsibility is often negated. Most if not all abnormality and sickness, emotional and physical hurt or disability, is essentially of the soul. That is, it involves one's self-concept, and can only be fully and permanently healed by spiritual means since transformation of thought about the self is ultimately needed. This transformation won't come if one is abetted or even made comfortable in the errors that produce the suffering. Nor if those errors are deliberately concealed or condoned by oneself or others.

Necessary Uncovering

Neither individuals nor society as a whole can effectively deal with problems without first seeing these problems and then comprehending their nature. For example, a care-giver may assume he's dealing with an adult's recurrent head and back pain as merely physical or stress-related. Efforts to relieve the sufferer will be temporary and largely unsuccessful until the source of the trouble is found out. Instead, he might need to put an end to that individual's unwitting re-play of terror-filled episodes of shock treatments administered when a teenager.

The difficulty in finding the source of the trouble is greater when some trauma or abuse occurs in childhood and the shock is repressed or the horror unrelieved, when no one helped the child make sense of what happened. Over the past decade there has been a literal explosion of information about the problems attendant upon abuse and exploitation of children. This "consciousness-raising" or heightened awareness has been necessary and remedial in itself.

It has been estimated that "one in three girls and at least one in seven boys in our society are sexually molested before the age of eighteen" (Ramsey in Pellauer 1991, 110). Further, "between 75 and 90 percent of the time, the abuser is an adult the (child) and those who would protect (that child) know and trust" (Fortune 1983, 166).

Sue Blume comments in the latest edition of <u>Secret Survivors</u> that most recent research "indicates that as many as 38% of women were molested in childhood." She continues: "...what is not remembered cannot be reported. It is my experience that fewer than half of the women who experience this trauma later remember or identify it as abuse. Therefore, it is not unlikely that <u>more than half of all women</u> are survivors of childhood sexual trauma" (1990, xxii).

Most counselors agree that early abuse is not a question of love or even sex, per se, but of power and control, of misuse of others and betrayal of their trust. The consequences of such abuse involve negation rather than validation, and a repression of feelings or memories that produces various destructive coping behaviors as well as a pervasive sense of self-doubt and self-hatred. It seems likely that this alone would account for the victim mentality with which many adults struggle.

Cultural attitudes or practices that foster repeated discrimination or denigration of any group would produce the same result: the creation of traumatic circumstances in which individuals feel helpless and unable to cope, lacking any frame of reference or informed standpoint from which to view their suffering.

Ignorance is bondage. What we as individuals or as a society don't know, or what we conceal and excuse, does have power to hurt us. Wrongs must be seen before they can be corrected. Nevertheless, most of us have to deal with considerable reluctance, including revulsion, disgust, horror, even to read about sexual desecration, betrayal, injustice, and violence, especially when directed at children. Obviously, more than education is needed. But education is often the first step to developing a stronger morality, a greater humanity, and a more spiritual outlook.

Factors other than ignorance adversely affect recovery. One factor that few authors address adequately is the tie between alcohol use and abuse of others. Most people are aware of the link between crime and drug use— particularly of the pervasive criminality associated with illegal drug trafficking and abuse. But few seem willing to admit the role of alcohol in violent or abusive incidents and the long-term consequences of these incidents, both within and without the family. In too many assessments of problems, alcohol or other drug use is seldom, if ever, even named.

More acknowledged are the ties between experiences of victimization and addictive, self-destructive behaviors, such as substance abuse, bulimia or anorexia, or compulsive eating, exercising, gambling, shopping or shoplifting. Even the perfectionism that masks an inordinate need for control, or internal replays of suffering and incapacity, or outbursts of anger and violence directed at others can grow out of experiences that violate.

There is never a valid excuse for abusiveness in any situation. Regardless of the social, economic, racial, or intergenerational aspects of the harm one suffers, or even the pervasive negative influence of a media culture in which brutality, sensualism, and materialism are often glorified, one cannot be excused from responsibility for one's own behavior toward others, or toward oneself. Any therapy, or theology, or program of rehabilitation that would absolve one of such responsibility does not facilitate either self-esteem or recovery, but fosters a kind of moral idiocy devoid of conscience or healthy shame.

Shame is unhealthy when the internal message is not "Something bad has happened," but "I am bad." Too often that is the consequence of early and secret abuse. Such shame causes feelings to be repressed, memories to be buried or frozen, and coping behaviors to develop.

A number of authors have dealt helpfully with the destructive consequences of shame (Bradshaw 1988, Fossum and Mason 1986, and Kaufman 1985, to name a few). Shame is "the self judging the self" (Fossum and Mason 1986, 40-41), and can profoundly damage a child's emerging identity, as well as erode and contaminate the adult's self-concept. Shame also engenders deep estrangement within the self and between the self and others, or the self and God, calling into question one's capacity for a healthy spirituality or a meaningful faith.

Damage to Faith and Spirituality

As Anne Carr explains it, "In relation to God, (spirituality) is who we really are" (1986, 49-58). Hence, the victimization that begets pervasive shame also produces a "sickness of the soul," a denial of hope and grace, coupled with chronic fear and self-contempt. It robs one of his true individuality.

Moreover, absence of caring or of understanding and support in the wake of victimization intensifies the harm. Carrie Doehring points out in her study of traumatization and God-representations that the church's silence, particularly with regard to childhood abuse and violence within the family, and its neglect of those who were abused has compounded their suffering (1993, 138).

Certainly, some aspects of traditional theological systems which promote suffering as both necessary and righteous, which support patriarchy and condemn sexuality, which build on the inherent sinfulness of humanity, and which emphasize God's sacrifice of His Son, need re-thinking in terms of their implications with regard to victimization.

Some feel there is even a danger in our society of swinging from the extreme of denial, secrecy, neglect, and either inadvertent or deliberate fostering of abuse, to the opposite extreme of becoming obsessed with victimization and thus inadvertently hindering recovery.

An ABC News Special entitled The Blame Game aired in 1994, pointed out many ways in which present attitudes and programs heighten rather than alleviate the consequences of victimization. Is our culture, in fact, fostering victimhood and dependency by rewarding victims and by robbing them of self-reliance and responsibility? Are we becoming "a nation of victims" by encouraging habitual blaming of others for one's often self-induced difficulties? Surely there is risk in fostering either self-deprecating or self-justifying attitudes.

Despite the caveat by Carol Travis in the New York Times that "almost any problem you have may be an indicator of abuse," and that "in the contemporary hysteria too many innocent adults are being unjustly accused" (New York Times Book Review, 3 January, 1993), anyone who has actually experienced violence and its subsequent traumatization does not pretend or invent its damaging consequences.

There is an important distinction to be made between those who have been victims of abuse and who continue, as a result, to assume a helpless, detached stance toward life, and those who identify themselves as victims simply because they feel cut off, hopeless, and inadequate to cope with life.

The severity of traumatic experiences may vary and their consequences may be heightened or lessened by a number of factors. Nevertheless, any individual who has, especially in childhood, suffered repeated inbreaking of what are termed the stimulus and repression barriers—the point at which one can process intense stimuli, or the barrier which prevents or limits unconscious material from flooding into consciousness—does not imagine the subsequent harm, or use it deliberately either as an excuse or a weapon to retaliate against others.

Reservations With Regard To Some Approaches

The wisdom and effectiveness of some approaches to recovery in vogue today—particularly the use of hypnosis to uncover repressed memories for those who want so desperately to find someone to blame or a reason for their private hells—is questionable. Memories are repressed because they are too painful to bear, and it often takes time and maturing, before one is ready to uncover and deal with them, or even express them to others. Moreover, memories are often frozen—that is, they represent the victim's perspective at the moment of trauma, and the individual must reach a point where he or she is able to reframe and revise these mental imprints from a more balanced and mature standpoint.

It is also of great importance that any counselor or therapist refrain from making assumptions or suggesting certain probabilities to those they treat, since each case is individual, and stereotyping is both wrong and cruel. The only thing worse than the abuse itself is a false accusation and its devastating effect on others. Still, if a family or organizational structure is healthy, and inter-relationships within it are normal and strong, free of hierarchical patterns of domination/submission or personal control, then such situations would, in all likelihood, never arise.

Obviously, concealment is in any perpetrator's self-interest. Some may feel, with reason, that preservation of the family, the church, or the community, and its "image" is all-important. But any covering of iniquity, of wrong-doing, or excusing of it, works against healing or normalization.

One of the appeals of 12-step programs is their emphasis on "hearing into speech" (Norton 1985, 205) those who have been silenced. The sharing of stories often develops needed insights and perspectives, while efforts to help others are, in themselves, therapeutic. But "support groups" can become addictive—that is, they can encourage dependency, and the constant rehearsing of trauma can work against one's eventual release from its consequences. After all, one can't go forward while persistently looking backward.

There is every reason to take exception to the assumption made in 12-step programs that one can never be free of addictive tendencies, or that one must always pass through certain stages in healing. Certainly, people progress toward normalcy by degrees. But not everyone needs to hit bottom in order to change, or to experience such emotions as denial, grief, and rage, or resort to bargaining in order to reach acceptance and attain freedom. Each situation remains individual, and most therapists stress the importance of dealing sensitively and in an unbiased way free of either pre-supposition or pre-judgment with each case.

Still, some general observations growing out of therapeutic practice have a certain validity, such as the common profile of an abuser as one who is likely to be "unable to have—or to take—his share of power in the real world or in his adult relationships" (Blume 1990, 35-36). It should be obvious that one who seeks to dominate or control others is himself deficient and insecure. But it would be a tragic mistake to presume that every such individual must necessarily be an abuser or even that one who has suffered abuse must necessarily repeat that behavior toward others.

Cloé Madanes, in a very helpful article on strategic family therapy, makes the point that: "One of the problems of victims is that they tend to define their whole personality as that of a victim" (1991, 410). In other words, the pervasive victim mentality that often results from early abuse will prevent normal maturation, and will manifest itself in irresponsibility, inability to retain a job, to make commitments, to relate to others in any but a superficial way. But she also maintains that when very bad things happen to people they develop a special quality of compassion that raises them to a "higher level of being."

Wayne Muller would agree, for he writes: "...adults who were hurt as children inevitably exhibit a peculiar strength, a profound inner wisdom, and remarkable creativity and insight. Deep within them...lies a profound spiritual vitality, a quiet knowing, a way of perceiving what is beautiful, right, and true... Seen through this lens, family sorrow is not only a painful wound to be...treated. It may in fact become a seed that gives birth to our spiritual healing and awakening" (1987, xiii-xiv).

This, of course, is the challenge and promise for those who would help into recovery any who struggle to find hope and meaning in their suffering. Sometimes well-meaning others—either wittingly or unwittingly—will actually stand in the way of a needed recovery. When a would-be helper becomes "co-dependent," that is, locked into some pattern of unhealthy relationship with the one in need, often out of guilt, false responsibility, or personal affinity, then he only prolongs the problem.

By excusing or covering up for another, usually out of pity or sympathy but possibly out of one's own need to be needed, and thus preventing that one from learning his own lessons or reaping the consequences of his own actions, a helper can actually inhibit a needed healing. It is seductively ego-enhancing to believe that only you can reach or help another—that no one else can suffice. From a spiritual standpoint, it substitutes person for God and inhibits another's essential maturing and awakening to his own true selfhood.

Again, deliberate hatred or malice, especially when hidden and unhandled, can be an obstacle to recovery. In the case of the man at the pool of Bethesda, if others had repeatedly prevented his getting into the pool when the water was troubled (the action he believed would heal him), or if he himself had become so envious of others' healings, so resentful of their progress, so filled with corrosive anger and bitterness that no one would help him, so focused on blaming others instead of improving himself, then such attitudes would act as a barrier to his own healing.

The Mind/Body Connection

It has been acknowledged by many in this century that Dr. Sigmund Freud developed some theories—particularly with regard to women and the effects of incest, as well as to religion—that were both distorted and incomplete. These notions have led to serious misunderstanding and produced damaging effects. Still, Freud did early acknowledge the relationship between thought and body. He promoted awareness in the medical/psychological field that feelings, attitudes and behaviors have a great deal to do with health.

Current research into psychoneuroimmunology leads to the conclusion that negative emotions directly affect the normal functioning of the body's immune system. This raises further doubt about the wisdom of abetting the release of such emotions as part of a therapeutic process. Does anger, turned inward as self-destructiveness, or outward in violence against society, have to be vented or can it be diffused and rendered harmless, or even transformed into a constructive determination to right wrongs for others?

As long ago as 1875, one prescient thinker concluded that sick thoughts evolve a sick body (Eddy 1906, 260). More recently, authors such as Surgeon Bernie Siegel of Yale,

Psychiatrist Joan Borysenko formerly of the Harvard medical faculty, the late Norman Cousins, whose own healing of an illness deemed incurable proceeded from a radical mental change, and a growing number of others emphasize the interrelatedness of thought and body. Medical admission that over 85% of all ills are psychosomatic in origin points to the fact that human thought or consciousness must be set right in order to improve physical health or body.

In Timeless Healing, Dr. Herbert Benson offers elaborate evidence that expectations and beliefs affect health, either positively or negatively (1996). The ability to elicit a feeling of being "saturated with love"—through prayer and faith and through bonding with others—he says, contributes significantly to healing. Progress also comes from what he calls "remembered wellness" (the placebo effect), and the relaxation response" (mental control of bodily states).

Further, Dr. Rudolph Ballentine, writing in Dawn Magazine, declares: "...what goes on in the mind structures the body." He continues: "How (the body) is shaped, how it functions, how it moves, how it works, the extent to which it works well, and the extent to which it breaks down...are all just expressions of what's going on in the mind." He concludes: "In essence, then, the body becomes a tool for self-discovery as well as a prod toward self-unfoldment. Illness can thus be seen in a positive light. When somebody gets sick it's not a tragedy; it's an opportunity" (Vol.8 No.1:13).

The Possibility Of Healing

Experience has led many to conclude that it's not the presenting trauma itself, but the individual's own reaction to it—what one makes of the injury, how one sees the experience—that gives it power to do harm. The opportunity, then, is to begin to understand that humanly "two-thirds of what we see is behind our own eyes"—derives from our own perspectives. Fear is the most obvious barrier to progress, and with it, ignorance or lack of awareness of what engenders fear and, more importantly, of the spiritual reality that transcends and dispels it.

The writings of many individuals imprisoned and tortured in war or in times of civil strife and unrest—for example the story of James Stockdale, the longest held and highest ranked prisoner who survived the Viet Nam war (Stockdale 1984)—make plain that, ultimately, it is not circumstances that victimize, but one's own sense of them. It has always been an inner and inviolable spiritual core that has enabled such victims to overcome extreme brutality and to turn from their suffering toward redemption.

Each survivor and each perpetrator must make the same choice Paul (who as Saul was an abuser) made: "...one thing I do, forgetting those things that are behind, and reaching forth unto those things which are before, I press toward the mark for the prize of the high calling of God in Christ Jesus" (Phil.3:13-14). One must determine to put away "childish things," (including immature attitudes and impressions) in order to know as he is known of God (I Cor. 13:11).

Clearly, some who have suffered early abuse survive relatively unaffected. Some are so damaged that they endure, and sometimes precipitate, repeated horrors and must rebuild their lives with great difficulty and at great cost. In some, the confusion and alienation persist and fester untreated and unmitigated for a lifetime.

That doesn't mean there is no answer to suffering. Rather, it signifies that some never find the answer, and some never have the courage or determination to seek it. There is an obvious danger in becoming so obsessed with some problem, or so entrenched in coping behaviors related to the problem, that one loses sight altogether of what is normal and right.

In such a case, pathology becomes idolatry (Jordan 1986). One ceases to realize that there is still a choice. One's thought turns so inward, and one identifies so totally with some difficulty or abnormalcy, that balance or perspective is lost. And imbalance or disarrangement is a good description of most mental (hence physical) disorders.

Sometimes individuals perpetuate their own difficulties because they're afraid not to. The sense of dependence becomes so ingrained or habitual that it is threatening even to consider change. Or it may seem easier to endure abnormalcy than to risk the pain of reopening old wounds in order to heal them. In our society, the one acceptable way to receive sympathy, attention, support, care, as well as to excuse one's self from responsibility is to be incapacitated or ill.

The fact remains that the inward always determines the outward—thought always governs experience. The need for an inner clarity, for an unclouded, undistorted spiritual perspective is paramount, for this perspective is the practical basis for all health and healing.

What brings someone to a point of willingness to change his perspective, to adopt a more spiritual outlook, to turn from his long-entrenched negative attitudes and be healed? Desperation can do it. When one has exhausted all other possibilities and realizes that he has become his own worst enemy, then he may be ready to listen. The humility that springs from a realization that you've been looking in the wrong direction, and that no one else can do for you what you alone must do—that no one else can "work out your salvation" for you—is another essential.

Certainly surrender of pride, willfulness, the false egotism that always argues for its own habits and indulgences, as well as the fear that paralyzes, are requisites for progress. Genuine repentance, a turning away from the false or negative and turning toward the genuine and positive, enhances receptivity to healing. Many chronic ills relate to extreme sensitiveness, to a high degree of reactivity, to the emotionalism that glorifies self, to an intense nervousness or insecurity that springs from lack of trust or faith in a governing Intelligence or divine Power. Sometimes what's needed is simply an admission to one's self that a mistake has been made, and that human will-power or strength won't suffice.

Several years ago, Thomas, a contractor from Florida, age 45, closed up his successful but stressful business and moved himself and equipment necessary to his work to a United States Territory in the South Pacific. His marriage had ended after several years of painful on and off separation. A lingering physical problem which he believed to be an intestinal virus seemed to be steadily worsening. His weight kept dropping. Life seemed empty and meaningless, full of conflict and confusion.

Once in his new location, he found breaking into the local construction market difficult. Within a few months, as the physical symptoms grew worse, he sought a medical diagnosis. A cat scan showed evidence of substantial internal malignancy, and the examining doctor advised immediate surgery in Honolulu. Without such treatment, the doctor concluded, his patient had only a few months to live.

Roused by this threatening prospect, Thomas made a choice to rely wholly on Christian Science treatment. He realized he'd been entertaining a great many negative concepts and conflicting feelings. In order to have more privacy to study and pray, he moved into an annex belonging to the Christian Science Society, and with difficulty got his things into the building in the heavy rains of an approaching typhoon. The weather forecast was for a mild storm. Nevertheless, he felt prompted to board up the windward side of the building.

He was startled from sleep by an inner voice ordering him to get up and put his electronics gear—computer copier, telephones—into plastic bags. He had just completed the task when most of the roofs of the main sanctuary and annex blew off. He was able to save a heavy box of records and other valuables, and when the eye of the storm passed over, to put up other reinforcements with the help of several neighbors.

The next morning revealed the building still standing, and with fairly minor damage. However, with the roof missing, serious rot and termite infestation of the timbers was exposed. Without first eliminating this inner rot, any repair to the roof wouldn't last.

Largely through Thomas' efforts, the needed reconstruction was accomplished in good order. Although the work took several months, not a single service had to be cancelled, and the buildings were left sound and strong— able to withstand five more typhoons the following fall.

Thomas' own healing took place shortly thereafter, lying in bed at the end of October with such intense pain that he realized he could no longer tough it out humanly, willfully. He knew he had to let go, trust God, and persistently defend himself against the internal storms that had created such havoc in his life. He began to do so.

That night he slept peacefully for the first time in many months, and since that time almost two years ago, he has fully regained normal weight, health, and strength. His business has prospered—his crew working overtime for more than a year. He has since married a fellow Christian Scientist whom he describes as a true companion and "soul mate." He feels that God has literally restored to him "the years that the locust hath eaten" (Joel 2:25), and has used him to bring courage, hope, and renewal to many others.

Our Eternal Relationship

No individual exists in isolation. The vast majority of ills dealt with by Christian Science practitioners in some way touch on close human relationships—or their absence— in a patient's experience. The underlying assumption on which such practice is based is that each one's ultimate relationship is with God the Creator, the Being in whose image we are made and whose purpose defines all existence. We can, therefore, rightly know ourselves only as we are known of God. And only the divine will—not genetics nor environment, though neither can be ignored—can be fundamentally determinative of one's selfhood.

The putting off of spiritually immature perspectives, the re-framing of inadequate myths or belief-systems, the resolving of sometimes deeply buried fears, inadequacies, and insecurities in order to be whole—in order to achieve the personal integrity or physical and emotional health that define one's God-created selfhood and so honor one's

Maker—is the goal for each individual in a Christianly scientific practice. And it is the road to recovery for everyone. With one in two marriages failing today, and with the needed lifting of the veil of secrecy that has so long existed with regard to family violence, it becomes important to acknowledge and validate right relationships and the joy that flows from them. Clearly, we must not become so engrossed with some problem that we fail to discern and appreciate the tremendous blessings inherent in community. As families fragment, one of the greatest problems of our time is simply disconnectedness, and the loneliness and depression stemming from it.

Marital oneness and mutual support, family harmony that provides proper and loving nurture of children, relationships both within and without the family that validate rather than denigrate, integrity and benevolence in all things: these make foundational contributions both to individual and societal health and stability. They are possible only within the context of each individual's relationship to God, or to a standard of values that is spiritually based.

Moral imperatives can never be attained without spiritual underpinnings, since the moral is the spiritual applied to human need. In the past few decades, an assault on Christian ethics and values by the media in general, together with the neutrality in personal morals of many churches and the pervasive secularism of our society, have given rise to a severe polluting of the mental environment. Thought-provoking discussions of the disastrous influence of the television and film industry can be found in Billingsley 1989, Hocking 1990, and Medved 1992.

Nowhere are the consequences of this pervasive attitude more vivid and threatening than in the AIDs crisis, from which more than 60,000 Americans have died. At the present rate of reported cases, 100 million people worldwide will be at risk from the AIDs virus by the year 2000 (Hocking 1990, 149-152). Ted Koppel on "Nightline" summed up the moral crisis of our time, and its answer, this way: "We have actually convinced ourselves that slogans will save us. Shoot up if you must, but use a clean needle. Enjoy sex whenever and with whomever you wish, but wear a condom. No! The answer is no! Not because it isn't cool or smart, or because you might end up in jail or dying in an AIDS ward. But no, because it is wrong."

And, because "no man is an island." In the world-wide-web culture of today, no individual's thoughts or actions remain unaffected or uninfluenced by the thoughts and actions of others. Problems are world-wide, so solutions must also be global. Asian women as well as American women know that humanity will perish without a vision of life as meaningful and worthy—without the hope that out of suffering and pain can come a world "defined by justice, wholeness, and peace" (Kyung 1992, 39).

When women and children around the world still live as property, used both for sexual and industrial purposes, when female circumcision is routinely practiced in Middle Eastern and African cultures, when bride burnings and widow immolations still occur, when daughters are sold as virtual sex-slaves by their parents, when women are valued in terms of the number of children they produce, when women provide two-thirds of the world's labor but reap only one-tenth of the world's wages, when 90% of college-educated women still start out in clerical tasks, and when physical and sexual abuse of women and children is tacitly sanctioned rather than condemned and outlawed, then it is

plain that the task of reforming and transforming attitudes
belongs to us all.

The Need For Spiritual Renewal

The goal of all pastoral work with those who have
been violated, or who see themselves as helpless victims,
must be nothing less than metanoia—the total and
irreversible change in attitudes that will do more than
mitigate suffering. The goal must be transformation of
thought, spiritual renewal and regeneration. As Paul put it:
"...be not conformed to this world: but be ye transformed by
the renewing of your mind, that ye may prove what is that
good, and acceptable, and perfect will of God" (Rom.12:2).

The highest art is preventive rather than curative.
Utter prohibition and annihilation of the attitudes and beliefs
that both result from and give rise to alienation from our
common divine Source, and that produce or allow the
aggression and oppression evidenced in either large scale
"ethnic-cleansing" or in isolated hierarchical infernos or in
private cruelties and abuse, must be our aim.

The editors of Christianity, Patriarchy, and Abuse
point out that some feminists today feel the Christian tradition
is "so entrenched in and undergirded by patriarchy that
without it, the very religion itself would disappear" (Brown
and Bohn 1990, xiii). While I disagree with that assumption,
I sympathize to some degree.

Every reform movement within the Christian Church
has sought to return to primitive or original Christianity—
to the gospels and the practical theology they embody. In
the earliest formulations of the Church, there was no "original
sin," no ecclesiastical hierarchy, no branding of women as

unclean and worthy of suffering, no exclusion of women from discipleship. Paul stated it: "There is neither Jew nor Greek, there is neither bond nor free, there is neither male nor female: for ye are all one in Christ Jesus" (Gal.3:26).

The time has come for theology to be freed from the Adamic myth and its consequences—from the concept of a man made of dust, cursed for his disobedience, shut out from the presence of God, and of woman as subservient to man. Fundamentally, we need to accept that this second account in Genesis is wholly allegorical, presenting the human misconception rather than the spiritual reality of creation as stated in the first chapter.

This misconception is what needs redemption, and the Christ or divine message Jesus brought to humanity as well as his example point out the way. It is a way of unselfed love, of forgiveness, grace, and compassion, which recognizes that the consequences of deliberate wrongdoing are far more damaging to the soul than the suffering of having been wronged. Jesus bore witness to the transcendant reality of a spiritual selfhood that remains forever inviolable, beyond the reach of human cruelty and wrath.

Far above mere human goodness or affection, such Christliness sees as God sees. It supplies the light and lens through which a transforming truth can be glimpsed. Christliness fulfils the role of an Interpreter, mentioned in Job, "to shew unto man his uprightness" and so provides the ransom—the means by which one held in some bondage regains his native freedom and wholeness as a child of God (Job 33:23-24). It breaks through self-erected and entrenched barriers and awakens the soul deadened in apathy and hopelessness, thus evoking the response or change that is the essence of healing.

Chapter Two

SPIRITUAL HEALING DEFINED

"I am The Lord that healeth thee" (Ex. 15:26)

One in three people in the United States today makes use of "alternative" treatments for health problems (Eisenberg, New England Journal of Medicine, January 1993). While most of this treatment costs far less than hospitalization or traditional medical methods, only a small fraction of it is covered by insurance.

Spiritual healing is listed among the most common alternate therapies, together with relaxation techniques, chiropractics, massage, and imagery. Others include: commercial weight loss, macrobiotic and other lifestyle diets, herbal medicine, self-help groups, energy healing, biofeedback, hypnosis, acupuncture, and folk remedies (Tye, Boston Globe 28 January, 1993, 1A).

Such findings should influence all legislative moves toward health-care reform. They indicate widespread dissatisfaction with a purely medical model of curing, despite its aggressive promotion and impressive technology. This dissatisfaction can only encourage those who feel that the transformation of thought which defines spiritual healing remains the ultimate answer to mankind's woes.

There is sufficient interest in such alternative methods that the National Institutes of Health recently created an Office of Alternative Medicine. Dr. Joe Jacobs, the Office's Director and a Yale-trained physician, is supportive of a "wellness" approach—preferring preventive to curative medicine. Jacobs admits to skepticism about medical decision-making, and declares that "in large part, medicine is an art, and not a science."

In fact, the best medicine is neither artifice nor educated guesswork. The best method of recovery involves fundamental concepts of self or being, of health, of suffering, of spirituality and prayer, of gender, of the whole human experience and its meaning, of obedience and responsibility. Most of all it involves a theology—an understanding of God, the I AM or Supreme Being, and the intimate, immediate, constant, relationship between the divine and human.

Such medicine is altogether mental and spiritual, since fundamentally the spiritual or inward determines the outward. Spiritual healing is a "gift" of the Spirit that is available to anyone who is willing to conform his thoughts and life to the demands of Spirit. Yet, while many people have experienced healing by spiritual means, only a few can explain it adequately or can practice it consistently. In an era as determinedly secular as ours has been, spiritual healing has evoked skepticism and resistance.

As the third millennium approaches, the spectacle and promise of materialism is failing. Despite tremendous advances in physical well-being and a standard of living sought by others around the globe, too many in the United States have lost their inner compass, their spiritual rigor and vision. What's most needed is spiritual renewal, including a Christianity that is scientifically provable, a theology that is fully practical and demonstrable.

Practical Theology Embodies Healing

One third of the Gospel records has to do with healing—with the overcoming of material limits of all kinds.

While a great variety of concepts and approaches today cluster under the heading of "spiritual," the healing that is Biblically-based is grounded in an understanding of God as Love, and an unshakable conviction of the power of this divine Love.

Certain non-medical practices tend to call into question the practice of spiritual healing in much the same way that early exorcists and diviners sought to emulate or even to discredit the works of Jesus' disciples (Acts 19:13-16). But genuine spiritual healing is fully effective, reliable, practical, as primitive Christianity proved.

Healing by spiritual means is too often regarded as mysterious, random, and unpredictable. Some experience of such healing rests on blind faith; some, on a mystical, altered mental state. Other practices stress ritual, notably laying on of hands. There still are widely divergent definitions of spirituality and concepts of prayer among those who seek meaning and relief from their ills. But the fact remains that most of the Christian churches are involved in some type of healing ministry.

Morton Kelsey, who, among others, has explored in his many published writings the role of healing in the Christian tradition, comments: "...the full message of Christianity has always offered the hope not merely of salvation in a world to come but of healing and wholeness in this world" (Kelsey 1986, 15).

Don Browning insists that all theology must be practical and that "the Christian message is primarily practical in nature" (Browning 1991, 67). In fact, theology, to be valid, must impact directly on human need and guide all human steps or actions taken to mitigate that need. The Word of God as lived and taught by Christ Jesus, and by prophetic figures both before and after his advent, is with power (Heb.4:12). God's Word relates specifically to the divine purpose at work in the world—to the redemption, reformation, restoration, transformation, that are the essence of healing.

The Word is "made flesh"—incarnated in regenerated thoughts and lives—whenever human experience is seen to be embraced by the divine. Such practical theology involves both immanence and transcendence. The power that heals is greater than we are—it is divine, not human. Yet, divine Love is present with us, even in the most tragic or apparently hopeless human circumstances. In the measure we open ourselves to this divine Reality—glimpse, accept, acknowledge, trust it— and then endeavor to conform our lives to it, it operates in our experience.

This is the prophetic method that is practical, effective, demonstrable, repeatable, hence, scientific—and that has been utilized for more than a century by a growing body of individuals. It is universal, not merely denominational, and it has had an undeniable effect in stirring and leavening all of human thinking.

Whatever changes our thoughts changes our experience. But the change that heals even bodily ills, all of which are fundamentally "psychosomatic," is nothing less than the deep, inner transformation that is irreversible because it awakens us to fundamental Truth. The experience of the man at the pool of Bethesda shows such healing to be an inner metamorphosis that involves spiritual transformation and the shedding of earth-bound perspectives, enabling us to see beyond the apparent to the actual.

The prevailing assumption that people can change a great deal or very little, depending upon their genetic

potential and limits and how enabling or disabling the
environment is, is not the basis on which Jesus healed.
Instead of assuming certain ills to be incurable, certain
problems unsolvable, or certain attitudes unalterable, Jesus
knew that "with God all things are possible" (Matt.19:26).

The healing that is based in such an understanding of
God does more than enable one to be accepting of
intergenerational predispositions or physical limitations. Such
healing is based fundamentally in a conviction that "God is
able to make all grace abound toward (us)" (II Cor.9: 8), and
that the power of the Holy Spirit is without measure.

Whatever moves us in the direction of health or
wholeness is salvation, or God's saving purpose manifest
humanly. To experience a movement from despair to grace
is the essence of the healing or transformation that is practical
theology. Does anything less have any claim to the name of
religion?

To re-frame harsh, tragic, or unjust experiences so
as to grow spiritually and learn lessons of love from them is
to be more than a victim, and more even than a survivor. It
is to be victorious, and potentially a "wounded healer" for
others. Power, ultimately, doesn't rest with persons or
circumstances but with one's own ability to discern what is
real or transcendant, and to live "as if" that truth alone is
actual and authoritative.

A Prophetic Approach Is More Than Holistic

The spiritual method that is prophetic is more than
holistic. It does more than acknowledge the mind/spirit/body
compendium, or even assert that the whole is more than a
sum of its parts. It is, in essence, a discerning of ultimate

reality that either corrects a human problem or lifts one out of it. Such healing results from glimpsing or discerning a truth, and then moving toward it, as defined by Canon Roy McKay in his 1974 address to the Guild of Pastoral Psychology (Lecture No. 177, 1974, 9).

Bible scholar Walter Wink declared in an article in the Christian Century: "A central aspect of Jesus' message was a critique of domination in all its forms, and the proclamation of an alternative reality, God's domination-free order, the reign of God" (27 April, 1994, 443). Spiritual healing springs from an acknowledgment of God's reign within us—from a recognition of and yielding to divine authority. If we allow any pathology to dominate us, to determine our outlook and govern our thought and actions, we are, in essence, making an idol. We are giving some problem the power that belongs to the Eternal Maker alone.

Whatever violates or desecrates our sense of who we really are and of what God is requires a spiritual solution. The permanent way to overcome human ills, to break their oppression and be free of victimization and its consequences, is to transcend these ills. Our need always is to take a prophetic viewpoint—a spiritual perspective. This perspective doesn't ignore or neglect the human need but meets that need in practical ways as the very evidence of Immanuel or "God with us."

An understanding of who one is in the sight of God and the ability to find meaning or purpose in one's suffering breaks the self-destructiveness of the victim mentality. Joan Borysenko puts it this way: "Healing is the rediscovery of who we are and who we have always been." She adds: "We are healed when we can grow from our suffering, when we can reframe it as an act of grace that leads us back to who we truly are" (Carlson and Shield 1989, 189).

If, in spite of failures, sharp disappointments and shattered fond dreams; if, in spite of the persistent mockery and pain of being either self-deluded and destructive or perhaps unwittingly uncaring of loved ones and unaware in their time of need; if, in spite of suffering and betrayal, one is able to grow spiritually and share with others the truths glimpsed through struggle, then there remains comfort and hope, and always the possibility of redemption. To participate in another's healing is to be healed.

All healing involves belief systems, as Droege makes plain in The Faith Factor in Healing (1991). All healing also involves a relational element, and an implicit anthropology, that is, a view about who we are existentially (humanly) as well as essentially (divinely or potentially). Healing also involves a sense of ultimate meaning or value—a perspective that goes beyond human seeming to eternal being.

Prophetic healing proceeds from insight and inspiration, including a divining or intuiting of the source of the suffering. The deep inner insecurity and fear, the fragmentation, the self-rejection and sense of shame that results in destructive compulsive/addictive behaviors and in physical disorders as well, have their roots in ignorance. Hence Christ Jesus' teaching: "Ye shall know the truth, and the truth shall make you free" (John 8:32).

This intuitive knowing involves more than an uncovering of some underlying or unconscious trauma, as necessary as that may be. Truth-knowing necessitates glimpsing the corrective spiritual fact, or the specific aspect of spiritual reality that pertains to the problem at hand. Truth-knowing involves seeing beyond the apparent to the actual.

The task of the prophet in Israel was to listen for, heed, and speak what God revealed. The priestly class, entrenched in ritual tradition and sacrifice and operating with a vested interest in prolonging the status quo, were often at odds with the prophetic. The priesthood—both medical and ecclesiastical—had then, and still has, a built in resistance to whatever challenges its authority.

Prophets are open to discovery and to dimensions beyond the obvious. They are visionaries. They are also fiercely moral and speak out with divinely derived authority against idolatry and injustice, against corruption and both individual and societal ills. Prophets also heal.

The man blind from birth whom Jesus healed "that the works of God should be made manifest in him," identified Jesus as a prophet. When challenged by the Pharisees, the man replied: "If this man were not of God, he could do nothing." Finally, he acknowledged Jesus as the Messiah, the Son of God, the one sent into the world for judgment "that they which see not might see" (John, Chapter 9).

It is a prophetic task to enable those who see not to see, to become aware or conscious of what was before unknown, and to be sufficiently discerning to transform the ordinary and recognize in it a divine purpose or meaning. The prophet also glimpses spiritual truth, sees as God sees, looks beyond physical evidence, gives loving recognition to and demands compliance with what is universal and true and Godlike in everything.

Here's one example of the effect of such prophetic seeing. About eight years ago, I was called by a grandmother, whose six year old grandson had fallen while playing outdoors. A stick he was holding had penetrated his eyeball. His mother rushed him to a nearby hospital, where she was told nothing could be done surgically. The doctor said the child's eye was so severely torn that there was little hope for the eye, and none for the child's sight in that eye. Nothing was done other than to place a patch over the eye, and the child was sent home.

The grandmother, with whom the mother and son were then living, refused to accept such a verdict, resting instead in the divine promise: "I will restore health unto thee, and I will heal thee of thy wounds..." (Jer.30: 17). She spoke to the little boy of God's present love and of his own safety, quieting his fears. In her prayers, she held fast to the intactness of the child's essential spiritual selfhood. This statement from the Christian Science textbook strengthened her resolve: "If it were possible for the real senses of man to be injured, Soul (God) could reproduce them in all their perfection; but they cannot be disturbed nor destroyed, since they exist in immortal Mind, not in matter" (Eddy 1906, 488).

When the doctor examined the boy a week later, perfect mending of the wound was evident. To the doctor's amazement and great joy, the child was soon back in school with no trace of injury or impairment of his vision. There is more to the story related to the healing. When the child was two, he had been abducted by his father and taken abroad. The parents, after a few years of a stormy inter-racial, inter-cultural marriage, had divorced, and on the occasion of a normal visitation, the father simply took the child to the airport and out of the country. There was no legal recourse for the mother.

After several weeks away, the father reluctantly brought the child back. His own mother insisted he do this for the child's welfare. She told him that a child so young needed his mother. This incident marked a healing in the family situation. Ill-will and suspicion were replaced with mutual kindness, and in the intervening years, there has been cooperation during the father's visits.

Knowing this background, when I was called by the grandmother about the eye injury, I insisted that the boy could not lose sight of good. He could not be emotionally or physically wounded by past events nor could the family be irreparably torn apart. His security and well-being rested with God, his eternal Father-Mother. He could not be a victim of circumstances or robbed of the sight God bestows.

Any such personal story of healing serves the same purposes as Kathryn Hunter points out in her article on the uses of anecdotes in medicine in <u>Perspectives in Biology and Medicine</u> (Summer, 1986, 619-630): 1) to challenge assumptions, 2) to instruct, 3) as justification for practice, 4) to illustrate or test the applicability of a covering (or governing) principle.

A central tenet of such healing is that causation is mental, and that the human body, and even human experience, only manifests what is in human thought. To change or correct the body, one must inform and change the thought that produces the body. Droege mentions studies of people with multiple personalities in this regard (1991, 10).

I do not take the position that one should never, under any circumstances, make use of temporary (temporal) means. Clearly, one's faith cannot be divided: one cannot "serve God and mammon" (Matt.6: 24). The primary resort must be to a power greater than our own, and this infinite Mind will guide us, if need be, to a right use of both temporary and eternal means (Eddy 1906, 444).

If our concept of being or selfhood is purely physical and material, then we would logically resort to purely physical (chemical, surgical) means for remedy or healing. As we begin to glimpse the interconnection between human thought and body, and the relationship between good health and spiritually based human thinking, we might utilize various long-range therapies or methods of improving human attitudes and outlook, including psychiatric and pastoral counselling.

But when we glimpse that being is fundamentally spiritual and that transformation of thought and body comes from yielding to what is spiritually real, then we will pray that our eyes be opened, and our hearts responsive to the divine Power that "forgives all our iniquities, that heals all our diseases, that redeems our life from destruction and crowns us with lovingkindness and tender mercies" (Ps. 103:3-4). Such prayer is ever efficacious. There really can be no failure in the effort to discern more of ultimate Truth.

Healing must be ministry, not industry; it must provide choice adapted to individual needs and perceptions, not impose monopoly. To be lasting, it must deal with more than symptomology. According to Carl Simonton, founder of the Simonton Cancer Center, "Illness is a negative feedback system: it is telling us what we need to stop doing" (Carlson and Shield 1989, 49). To medically remove symptoms or to merely go for the "quick fix" can, then, be detrimental to the modification or change of thought we most need. It can drive the unchallenged fear or trauma further underground.

Appropriate, loving care for human needs is always requisite and should be provided. Practical wisdom always accompanies prophetic insight. Surgeon Bernie Siegel initiates treatment by asking patients what they get out of being ill, and that is an honest point of beginning whenever one seeks recovery. At some point, individuals must mature into an understanding of what constitutes health and take adequate responsibility for their own health-maintenance. And it is with divine care and guidance that this journey is made.

Moreover, it is to divine authority that we appeal and upon which we depend. This authority rests in Scripture and its spiritual meaning, and in our own experience of God's grace. Jesus' life illustrated God's promises fulfilled. The important thing is that we be attuned to the divine perspective—to what God is and wills or causes to be. The relational element that is essential for healing is one's relationship with God. Only out of this at-one-ment with the divine do right human relationships and normal health and activity flow.

Whatever the spiritual fact is, the human sense of things must ultimately conform to it. It is as hard for us as for the Apostle Paul "to kick against the pricks" (Acts 9:5). To the extent that God's will or law is sought, understood and obeyed, such conforming will take place, either in full measure or by degrees, here and now.

There is a <u>Christian</u> science (that is, a Christianly scientific approach to healing and redemption) that is prophetic in nature and that transcends medical, biological or psychological science. This effective method of recovery involves a human and divine coincidence wherein the human sense of things is brought into conformity to what is divinely real or valid.

A Presbyterian chaplain in a large hospital puts it well: "Spiritual healing does not involve a suspension of

God's laws. I do not like to hear spiritual healing equated with 'miracles.' This puts such healing in the realm of the extraordinary and supernatural... Effective prayer for healing taps into the existing spiritual world which is part of the (divine) order of things..." (Keller 1969, 227).

God's Image Is "Made Whole"

Beyond either a biomedical model or a bio-psycho-social model of the individual stands each individual's spiritual status as a child or image of the divine Being. This individuality is "made (created) whole"—and remains perfect, unharmed, intact, sound, indestructible. This eternal fact of being is not simply one facet among many. It is the underlying reality or spiritual basis of all existence. God's message to the prophet Jeremiah conveys this underlying reality: "Before I formed thee in the belly I knew thee; and before thou camest forth out of the womb I sanctified thee..."(Jer.1:5).

The most important thing we can know about illness or suffering is that God isn't the cause of it, nor is it in accord with the divine will or purpose. Therefore, it has no ultimate validity or spiritual "reality." Moreover, through spiritual insight, through some glimpse of our own or another's true nature or selfhood in the likeness of the divine, we can translate any trauma, any victimization or suffering, into a creative opportunity, and thereby do the works Jesus promised we should do.

The following account is one of many included in Robert Peel's Spiritual Healing in a Scientific Age. The personal "stories" or histories selected for publication in his book all had medical diagnosis and/or verification of healing.

A California couple was asked to adopt a just-born infant with multiple birth defects and severe handicaps. As Christian Scientists, they refused to accept the medical prognosis that the infant would not survive more than six to eight months. The problems included unformed vocal cords, a damaged heart, defective bone structure, and cerebral palsy. The baby was considered too frail for corrective surgery. At the time their affidavit was sworn in 1983, all of these problems had been healed. The son was then fully grown, healthy, married, and employed as a plumber.

In a lengthy interview, the wife remarked: "In the beginning we did think human love was going to be enough. When we first knew we were going to take this little child into our home...we thought we could just love him out of anything. And we had to learn that divine Love...does the healing. And that takes a lot of praying, forgiving, it takes patience, it takes listening. It takes being directed and allowing yourself to let God's will and not your own unfold...You have to love yourself too...to see yourself the way God sees you."

There is much of the prophetic in the way this couple viewed their child over the years of his rearing. They never saw him as pitiful or disabled nor doubted his capacity to develop in a normal way. Clearly, they were instruments of transformative divine Love, and the boy came to view his experience as a working out of God's purpose and a blessing. His story is a beautiful illustration of the "presence and power of God embracing, redeeming and healing—even while transcending—the whole human enterprise," as Peel describes it (1987, 54-63).

"...the health of any child is inextricably bound to the quality of emotional (and I would add, spiritual) support provided by the parents...The ability of the family to respond and the manner in which its members choose to do so can be the decisive element in how a child learns to work with and overcome a chronic illness," writes Robert Massie, Jr. in a public policy paper on the chronically ill child (1982, 4). The same conclusion would apply to any developmentally handicapped child, or to one who had suffered severe trauma.

Those who work with individuals in need often find themselves working with whole families or other social groupings. J.L. Framo, for example, contends that when a child needs help the entire family should be treated. He insists that pathology in one member is a symptom of family, often intergenerational, dysfunction (1984).

This coincides fundamentally with the imperative in Christian Science practice to deal with the parents' state of thought—that is, to resolve the fears or projections in the parents' thinking—in every child's case.

No one exists in isolation. Sometimes an entire context needs to be set right. But whatever changes one individual in a context will change the whole—every relationship of which one is a part will thereby be changed. The hope is that any individual who has suffered and been healed will, by his or her example, give encouragement to others. One's own light will shine.

Healing Is More Than Cure; Health Is More Than A Physical State

Because genuine healing always involves inner change, it is more than just physical repair or cure of matter. By the same token, health is more than merely a physical or bodily state. The body is a human concept, a metaphor for what goes on in consciousness. Treatment, then, can't be based solely on the physical evidence but should not ignore such evidence.

A good illustration of this point appears in <u>Power Healing</u>, which includes the experience of a pastor who initially resisted and disparaged Christian healing but who has since taught graduate courses and led international conferences on the practice of such healing.

His wife discovered a substantial lump in her breast. As she prayed over the problem she became aware of deep-rooted feelings of abandonment and loneliness arising out of circumstances in her childhood. What had precipitated the problem was release of a significant number of the membership of their church to form another Fellowship some distance away. Included in those who left were the wife's sister and brother-in-law. She glimpsed that suppressed hurt feelings, bitterness and resentment at the change had manifested themselves as a lump. Once this was seen, husband and wife prayed together. As she was freed of resentment, within a few days the lump vanished (Wimber 1987, 78-79).

Health is really wholeness or holiness. That doesn't mean, however, that suffering or ill-health are necessarily to be equated with unholiness. Sin, or the belief in a power apart from God, or the assertion of human will or of a material self separate from God, brings suffering, but not all suffering is the result of sin.

Some suffering is the result of deliberate malice, envy, or hatred. Some arises from circumstances or social contexts. To share in Christ's suffering or take up the cross, I feel, means to bear with patience the world's enmity and help to redeem it. As Victor Frankl makes plain, there can be no excuse for not acting as though one is the loved of God (Frankl 1962).

The Promise Of Suffering

Is suffering, then, simply to be endured? Certainly not. Some feminist writers today question the role of traditional Christian "virtues" in recovery from trauma, particularly that of sexual abuse. Sheila Redmond, for example, points out that the value placed on suffering and even martyrdom in traditional Christianity can be used to deny the destructiveness of violence and abuse. She sees even forgiveness as instilling a sense of unworthiness and guilt in the victim, and the concept of filial obedience used to invest adults, particularly adult males, with unquestioned authority (Brown and Bohn 1989, 70-80).

The promise in any suffering is that we learn from it, and that through our own experience and hope "the love of God is shed abroad in our hearts..." Paul even wrote to the Romans of glorying in tribulation, "knowing that tribulation worketh patience; And patience, experience; and experience, hope: And hope maketh not ashamed..." (Rom. 5:3-5).

It is noteworthy that the Greek root of the word tribulation means " to sift," that is, to separate out tares from wheat, fable from fact, wrong from right. Paul was well-suited to conclude that "we must through much tribulation enter into the kingdom of God" (Acts 14:22).

But Paul didn't simply endure suffering or so counsel others. He confronted suffering, especially the suffering that comes from ignorance of the saving Truth, and he healed those who were suffering. Though Paul was never relieved of his own "thorn in the flesh," God's promise: "My grace is sufficient for thee..." (II Cor.12:7-9) was fulfilled in his life. As a result of his transformation on the road to Damascus, Paul viewed Jesus' life and teaching as the remedy for Adam, for the material and mistaken view of man as sinful, fallen, and cursed.

Jesus' mission was to express the divine nature or Being, to glorify his Father or Source. He was imbued with compassion, grace, and forgiveness but was strong in his rebuke of ecclesiasticism, of hypocritical authority with its arrogance and self-righteousness. This called down upon him the wrath of the Pharisees. Yet, his reply to Pilate was: "Thou couldest have no power at all against me, except it were given thee from above..." (John 19:11). He acknowledged that, no matter how it appeared, only God had jurisdiction over him, and only God's purpose could be worked out in him.

The wonder of Jesus' sacrifice is that it illustrates for all who suffer cruel injustice that, even if hope, faith, and life itself are hung on some cross, one can come down from that cross through forgiveness and triumph over it through love. "They know not what they do" (Luke 23:34) pertains to all who injure others ignorantly or deliberately. They know not what an offense they are committing against God or what expiation will be required of them before redemption can come.

For most of us, the change that is transformation comes gradually and often through the challenges we face. Not that God punishes, condemns or afflicts—sends crisis, tragedy, or brokenness to humanity, nor even allows or sanctions such harm. Instead, divine Truth, or some glimpse of what is spiritually real, enables us to transcend any crisis, gives us the wisdom to turn it into opportunity and restore to wholeness whatever seems impossibly fragmented or damaged. Nothing but divine Love can give the courage, resilience, and strength needed to combat injustice and to change for the better both attitudes and experience.

Such change can take place at many levels. Efforts to provide safe havens for battered women and children and maintain rape crisis centers or 24-hour "hot lines," to strengthen law-enforcement interventions in domestic violence situations and educate in mediation techniques can help to transform a violent society. Fundamental changes in patriarchal doctrines and in corporate and business policies toward women and minorities can alter discriminatory attitudes. Greater participation by all groups in political decision-making can transform political systems. Even the sordid, violent, prurient, and degrading can fail to find an audience and so be abandoned by the image-makers. All these changes have an important part to play in transformation of the environmental and social context in which victimization occurs.

But all such efforts will fall tragically short and prove woefully inadequate unless undergirded by the conviction that God is not a man, but a divine Spirit manifest in both men and women—defined by both fathering and mothering qualities, and served equally, even though uniquely, by both men and women according to their individual gifts.

Whether socially or individually, it is always some phase of wrong thinking that is in need of redemption. It is always some misconception of the divine nature or violation of it that causes suffering. And it is always through honoring that nature by expressing its fundamental goodness and transforming love that humanity is freed from anguish and torment.

Sin and its torment always involve alienation from God, a misunderstanding of what is divinely true, a mistaken sense of one's self, whereas salvation is the progressive awakening to one's God-created wholeness. Salvation is the Christ, Truth, or true idea and nature of God repairing the breach, and restoring "paths to dwell in" (Isa.58:12).

Genuine health is the effect of God understood. In Tillich's words, it is "man reconciled and thereby re-established in his essential and created harmony" (Tillich 1957, 41). Health is a condition of mind not matter, of the "spirit that quickeneth" (John 6:63), not of the flesh. Moreover, health is the state in which the divine Being and its manifestation dwells, and is a response to the divine will or law, an expression of divine blessing or grace.

Health is manifest outwardly in purity, order, harmony, balance. Healing, therefore, is not an event but a homeostasis-like process by means of which health is constantly renewed and maintained. Are mortals, then, always responsible for the ills they suffer? No. But ultimately, they are responsible for the way they confront and deal with those ills.

Self-acceptance and self-esteem and the healthy states they engender arise fundamentally from an understanding of one's self as the beloved of God. Recognition that one's spiritual selfhood made in God's image remains whole and holy—intact and undamaged, subject to no inherent or hereditary weaknesses, no cruel deprivations, no invasive traumatizations, brings healing when nothing else can. What is authentic and unalterable about any of us is our Godlikeness.

To suppose that the effects of some violation can never be mitigated or healed and that an offense can never be forgiven; to accept that the self-contempt and shame, or the rage and destructive behavior engendered by abuse can never be transformed but must be fixed in an individual's psyche and even transmitted through attitudes and behaviors to subsequent generations is to make an idol out of the abuse. It is to make the abuse of greater importance and to give it greater power than God.

Because we are the beloved of divine Love, we must inevitably awaken to this fact. This is the proclamation that speaks "back into the world of ambiguities from the place of unconditional love" (Nouwen 1992, 28-31). If belovedness were not the fact, we couldn't hope to understand or experience it. But because it is, we must.

The prayer that heals, then, "is not asking God for love; it is learning to love, and to include all mankind in one affection. (It) is the utilization of the love wherewith (God) loves us." Mary Baker Eddy continues: "Prayer begets an awakened desire to be and do good. It makes new and scientific discoveries of God... It shows us more clearly than we saw before, what we already have and are; and most of all, it shows us what God is" (Eddy 1891, 39).

Chapter Three

SPIRITUALITY AND PRACTICE

"To be spiritually minded is life and peace" (Rom. 8:6)

On a global or even national scale, few people feel themselves truly beloved. Many struggle just to survive. Some may feel fortunate, blessed with family affections, comfortable circumstances, stable health, meaningful activity. Others feel deprived or bereft of their deepest desires, often lacking basic necessities, sometimes anxious or troubled, seldom secure. Where can inner peace and security be found? The answer has to lie in an understanding of our fundamental spirituality.

What It Means To Be Spiritual

The essence of spirituality is goodness. Those qualities Jesus pointed to as blessed (Matt.5:3-12): meekness, patience, charitableness, forgiveness, peaceableness, righteousness, purity, constitute spirituality, and are indispensable to mental and physical health.

Their opposites: pride, impatience, selfishness, resentment, anger and violence, hatred, dishonesty, self-will and the self-gratification of sheer sensualism, have a contrary effect, leading to physical and moral death. The opposite of spirituality is materiality; that is, being materially-minded, occupied with fleshliness or worldliness, driven by appetite or passion.

To be spiritual is to be sincere, devout, righteous, moral, right-minded, pure in heart, holy, Christly. How do we distinguish genuine spirituality from whatever would counterfeit it, especially the hypocrisy that gives an appearance of good but lives in opposition to it, or that serves evil in the name of good?

We know the spiritual by its fruits, which Paul defined as: "love, joy, peace, longsuffering, gentleness, goodness, faith, meekness, temperance" (Gal.5:22-23). Paul also declared: "...to be carnally-minded is death; but to be spiritually minded is life and peace" (Rom.8:6). There's no escaping the fact that what we sow, we reap. If we sow to the flesh (to physicality, materiality, sensuality, earthliness), we reap corruption; but if we sow to the Spirit, we reap life everlasting (Gal.6:7-8).

Genuine spirituality does not correspond to mysticism or asceticism. It isn't "other-worldly" or paranormal, impractical or oblivious to human needs. It doesn't relate to the esoteric, the psychical, or to the notion that departed "spirits" or even "demons" can control or use as mediums other human personalities. Spirituality transcends ecclesiasticism or religiosity.

Because God is Spirit, infinite, omnipresent, omnipotent, there can be no evil spirit, that is, nothing ultimately real, present, powerful or operative that is contrary to the nature of God.

Jesus gave to humanity an unparalleled example of spiritual sonship. Jesus' spirituality, his recognition of who he was and his living in accord with that status, enabled him to do the healing works which validated his mission. His purpose was to bear witness to the truth of being, thus honoring his God and our God. He acknowledged: "I can of mine own self do nothing" (John 5:30). It was the Father dwelling in him, the Spirit with which he was imbued, that enabled him to overcome the world.

To follow Jesus and do the works he did, and to practice a Christianly scientific method of healing, requires the conforming of our own thoughts, energies, attitudes, behaviors, and desires to a spiritual standard. Only thus can we consistently employ the protection and blessing of divine law.

By implication, the spiritual—our true selfhood— is fetterless, ageless, fearless, innocent, inspired, strong, calm, courageous, joyous, whole. To be spiritual is to experience God-given dominion and freedom. Spirituality involves an awareness that one's God-created selfhood is ultimately beyond the reach of cruelty, violence, or chance. Real spiritual being is exempt from material or fleshly limitations. It is fundamentally and irreducibly incorporeal, made in the image of God, and not subject to violation or desecration, whether random or deliberate, ignorant or intended.

It is spirituality that imparts wisdom, courage, vision, and love, that enables one to survive and overcome cruelty, brutality, misfortune, abuse, and to help others do so as well.

To be prophetic is to see from a spiritual perspective. It is to "discern the spiritual fact of whatever the material senses behold" (Eddy 1906, 585). The spiritually-minded see from another dimension, from the standpoint of ultimate reality. They judge "not according to the appearance" but righteously (John 7:24).

Spiritual-mindedness implies being in the world but not of it. Those who are spiritually-minded have an instant rapport with one another. They empathize and communicate regardless of language, religion, culture, race, or class. In fact, spirituality is the underlying commonality of all people.

The Bible reminds us: "It is He (God) that hath made us, and not we ourselves" (Ps.100:3). All people share one divine Source of all blessedness, one heritage. That doesn't homogenize humanity into a single mass or eliminate individuality and uniqueness, since God is infinite and must be infinitely expressed. But it means all can unite on the basis of one Creator, one fundamental law or divine Principle of being, one universal Love. Individual at-one-ment, accord, or harmony with the Power greater than ourselves alone undergirds justice and peace.

The genuine self-esteem that is foundational to mental and physical health is attained only in the measure of one's spirituality. Self-esteem doesn't come through self-assertiveness or egotism, nor from ethnic pride, academic distinction, economic success, or even nationalism. The recognition of one's true status as the loved of God is the only lasting basis of satisfaction, dignity, and self-worth.

That's why shame endangers spirituality. It negates rather than affirms true selfhood. It begets a victim mentality because it entrenches one in the sense of himself as merely mortal—hence, helpless, valueless, meaningless, destined to oblivion.

Our goal, then, must be to see spiritually and "walk" that way: to live, think, behave, work from the standpoint of our at-one-ment with God, Spirit. This goal necessitates our "setting our affections on things above" (Col.3:2), impelling us to "come out from the material world and be separate" (II Cor.6:17)—to separate from our thinking all that is worldly or materially based.

Separateness doesn't imply or require monasticism. Nor does it exclude others or negate their needs. There is no self-righteousness but great humility involved in an unceasing effort to be Godlike, to stay attuned to the divine Mind, and to engage in the "habitual struggle to be always good" that is unceasing prayer (Eddy 1906, 4). But there is usually a backlash, a worldly antagonism or resistance, to be met and handled.

The World's Hatred Of Spirituality

Jesus admonished his followers: "If the world hate you, ye know that it hated me before it hated you" (John 15:18). But then he added: "...be of good cheer; I have overcome the world" (John 16:33). Aggressive materialism will seek to crucify the Christ in each of us in the measure of our demonstrated spirituality. Often it will strike at whatever is dearest to our hearts, at whatever point we seem most vulnerable.

The materially-minded are discomforted by spirituality, suspicious of it, sometimes envious of it, always antagonistic to it. The entrenched "powers" of this world resist and fear genuine spirituality. Often what appears as a personal attack is really just the attempt of animality to render our spirituality ineffective, to so absorb us in our own pain as to make us of little use to others.

Animality's greatest effort is to lessen our love, to make our love conditional, to defile, pervert or distort our sense of what love is, or even make us afraid to love, and so separate us from the divine Love that alone heals. This point was made in a letter written by Mrs. Eddy to a student and republished in 1936: "Love is the only and all of attainments in spiritual growth. Without it, healing is not done and cannot be either morally or physically. Every advanced step will show you this until the victory is won and you possess no other consciousness but Love divine" Christian Science Sentinel 28 March 1936, 590).

This divine Love imbued Jesus' life, his teachings, and his healing work, and enabled him to overcome the hatred his spirituality aroused. He taught his followers that we are blessed to be "persecuted for righteousness sake" (Matt.5:10-12). The world's hatred of good is the cross, and we all must bear it in some way. When we do, we win and wear the crown (Eddy 1906, 254).

Not that Jesus advocated martyrdom. His own sacrifice illustrates the powerlessness of evil to destroy good, of hatred to annihilate love, of cruelty and violence to do away with life. Referring to his coming crucifixion and resurrection, he said: "For this cause came I unto this hour" (John 12:27). He was showing mankind the immortality, the indestructibility of spiritual selfhood.

To remain actively aware of that selfhood, true to it, and conscious of God's presence with us is of far greater importance than any human circumstance could ever be. To be imbued with the Spirit and with its power, even in small degree, matters more than all else. Whatever wars against this spiritual awareness or would operate as a constant pull against it must, therefore, be abandoned or rectified.

When Jesus spoke of our need to cut off the right hand and pluck out the right eye (Matt.5:29-30), he was symbolizing the urgent need to separate from ourselves those demoralizing attitudes or behaviors, those flaws of temperament, those tendencies to focus on self, even personal will, pride, or egotism, that would attempt to defile our

Christliness. Sooner or later each of us must choose to leave whatever hinders our pursuit of Christ—the truth of God and man.

Today there is great reluctance to use the term "sin" or even to speak out against practices that are immoral, abusive, dishonest, spurious, wrong. Tolerance has become the approved or "politically correct" attitude. But toleration can't come at the expense of dignity, rectitude, or even sanity. Liberty can't become license.

The reign within us of harmony, health, peace, joy is not accessible except through our return to innocence, affection, purity, trust, humility, obedience to the laws of God. As a culture, we almost seem bent on destroying these child-like qualities as though we resent them or regard them as obstacles to our self-fulfillment. Yet, they constitute our true selfhood and our protection.

We must heed the Master's warning: "Except ye...become as little children, ye shall not enter into the kingdom of heaven...whoso shall offend one of these little ones...it were better for him that a millstone were hanged about his neck, and that he were drowned in the depth of the sea...woe to that man by whom the offence cometh" (Matt.18:3-7).

Jim's experience illustrates the antagonism and hatred directed at spirituality, especially at children of promise. Jim was a child of the 1960's. In his early years, his family lived in a neighborhood that was very suspicious of and antagonistic to his religion. Older children in this neighborhood, reflecting their parents' attitudes, treated him hatefully, abusively, physically tormenting him and ridiculing him with spite and vindictiveness. As a result, there developed in his thinking a dichotomy between what he was

secretly experiencing and the religious teachings of his
family.

Jim early developed an intense desire to please
others, to be accepted and not rejected, to be included—at
almost any expense to his comfort, health, well-being, and
true identity. As a result, well into his teens, he lived what
he calls "a precarious balance" between a good life with his
parents and a hidden, disobedient, sensual life with friends.
Big for his age and gifted with a certain charisma as well as
many creative talents, Jim found many aspects of the world
intriguing.

The family made several business-related moves, the
happiest of which was a two year period on the West Coast,
where Jim found compatible friends and for the first time
felt happy, secure, normal, and at peace. Abruptly, the
company where his father was employed was bought out
and to Jim's great dismay, his dad accepted an offer that
necessitated their return East. Jim was enrolled in a very
conservative private school where he stood out as an athlete
and leader.

There, in the Ninth Grade, Jim was introduced to
drugs and to an intense sexual affair with a young woman
who was also intimately involved with others. At the same
time, he was approached by a man who taught at the school,
and began a several year homosexual involvement with this
teacher. Jim felt flattered and compromised. At the same
time he developed a physical problem that caused him great
embarrassment and stood in the way of the career he hoped
to pursue. Finally for Jim the situation was completely out
of control, and he dropped out of school several months
before graduation.

After some months of living in a dangerous environment, Jim returned home, took his GED, and was accepted at college and ultimately graduated. His family was proud of this accomplishment, and Jim credits their prayers with steering him safely through the intervening years. Still, there were many unresolved problems. He could see the need for a "spiritual fortress" as he terms it, but wasn't able to maintain an effective mental defense. He states: "Somewhere in all the craziness and ugliness of the drugs, sex, drinking and so on, was a sincere, heartfelt individual who really loved life and people... There was this emerging...desire to bring more uplift to life and to the people around me."

In the midst of many pressures related to Jim's developing career, his father became seriously ill and within a few months passed on. In his grief and fear of being alone with his feelings, Jim turned the wrong way. He became addicted to heroin. He lost whatever self-confidence he had developed. To him, everything seemed like "a dead end of immorality, unethical business practices, deceit, and a very shallow outlook on life and its purpose."

He agreed to go to a treatment center. "After all the social demands of doing what the 'in-crowd' did, and feeling that this was the only way to communicate with people and be accepted, here I was isolated, ashamed, humiliated," Jim wrote. He was also at the threshold of awakening—of coming to himself, like the Prodigal.

But there were still problems. Career-wise, nothing seemed to "jell." Another encounter with his high-school girlfriend, who had already been once married and divorced, led nowhere. Finally Jim reached the point of realizing that it wasn't "person" that was going to make his life complete, but a better understanding of his own true selfhood as God's likeness, perfect, whole, satisfied.

He began working with a Christian Science practitioner. He wrote: "The love that was shown towards me by that practitioner was so helpful in overcoming the nagging nightmare of thinking I had to drink to feel comfortable or socially accepted." Jim began to realize that he wasn't a helpless mortal condemned to live in sin and sorrow all his life. Every vice he'd been involved with, addicted to, or felt included in doing just disappeared. Jim was free and unafraid. His life has been made new, even to the point of being able to help others see through numerous falsehoods about themselves.

Relationship Between Spirituality And Sexuality

If spirituality has to do with who you really are, then anything that causes confusion about this real identity, anything that breeds a sense of self-rejection, or subverts your sense of yourself, is really an attack on your fundamental spirituality.

Psychology today insists that our relationships with others, particularly close family ties, shape us. Psychology even suggests that we are driven into adult relationships out of a need to replicate childhood experiences or patterns that are often abnormal or dysfunctional. But each individual's fundamental and determinative relationship is with God. When you feel yourself begotten and loved of God, and cherish your own innate spirituality, then you are unlikely to struggle with problems of sexual orientation or with the destructive sensualism that is so exploited in our society today.

In its original meaning, the word sex simply implies kind, gender, or sort. Sexuality refers to manhood or womanhood, to masculine or feminine character. It is widely recognized today that every individual includes both masculine and feminine qualities, and that marriage is often a search for the completeness which union of these qualities brings. To accept one's God-created sexuality, to express masculinity or femininity in a normal, healthy, enhancing way, is to honor the Creator. That's why the abusiveness that violates or calls into question sexual identity is really an offense against God.

My own experience in practice is that most sexual perversions have their origin in early abuse. In fact, many boys misused by men, or deprived of normal companionship with a father, or drawn by circumstances into an unhealthy enmeshment with the mother, spend much of their lives yearning and searching for an affirmative relationship with a man. Women who find it difficult to relate sexually to a man and are drawn to other women for intimacy often have suffered early abuse—sexual, physical, or emotional—at the hands of a man.

Despite the argument that homosexual orientation is immutably fixed, sometimes pre-natal or "in the genes," Ethel Person affirms in her article, "Sexuality as the mainstay or identity," that human sexual behavior depends much more on learning and experience than on hormones and genetics. She also insists that the crucial steps in psychosexual development and gender differentiation occur very early and that such orientation is established by the third year of life (Person 1980, 605-630).

Sexual performance is generally believed to be far more important to personality development for men than for women. Therefore, it is not unlikely that early sexual abuse has more damaging effects on boys than on girls.

Today, there is a well-funded, vigorous political thrust for homosexual rights, promoted via the arts, media, entertainment, and fashion industries. It becomes very difficult for an individual to break away from the entire social, economic, political structure that has evolved in defense of homosexual practices. But if homosexuality or any sexual abnormalcy results from unresolved trauma, if it produces such devastating afflictions as AIDS, and if it has not only personal but social consequences—perhaps for more than a generation—then should it not be regarded as an abnormalcy to be healed rather than a "natural" choice to be defended?

I have never encountered anyone struggling with such a sexual orientation problem who is happy or satisfied. Much self-hatred is involved in abnormal behavior, as well as hatred of the other sex. Moreover, any perversion inevitably discolors and distorts other aspects of one's experience, leading to confusion, deception, and ultimately, despair.

What about physical closeness in marriage? It is a natural outcome of spiritual oneness. But without such oneness, physical intimacy can become unsatisfying, degrading, hypocritical, even dangerous. That's why those who put sexual intimacy first run the risk of endangering the oneness of heart that is all-important in an honest, long-term, committed relationship.

Deep, intense feelings of pleasure and delight come from the thought that prompts them: from both partners' total openness to one another, from shared affection and mutual trust, not from domination or submission, or from sheer physical sensation.

Sexual intimacy can best be thought of as a means of communication, a type of body language, by which the deepest sense of tenderness, commitment, warmth, esteem and acceptance can be conveyed. Such feelings are often hard to verbalize, and it is wonderfully strengthening and reassuring that they can be conveyed in marriage and so protected and nurtured.

On the other hand, selfishness or sensualism weakens and impoverishes. Lust or sensuality is synonymous with appetite, biological urge or drive, fleshliness, lewdness, animality, greed. Sheer physical attraction is mesmeric; it may be infatuation, but it is not love. Seductiveness is always exploitative, manipulative. It preys on those of uncertain confidence in their own manliness or womanliness.

The August 15, 1994 issue of Time magazine boasted the word "Infidelity" on its cover, with the added suggestion: "It may be in our genes." The feature article, entitled "Our Cheating Hearts," reported that, according to current evolutionary psychology, it's "natural" to commit adultery or to sour on a mate. Such theory stresses how "inhospitable" the current social environment is to monogamy, and claims that shifting attitudes toward a mate are the handiwork of natural selection. The article's basic assumption is that men and women are animals driven by biological urges toward the sole purpose of reproduction.

But is that anyone's true identity? Shall we not, rather, "look unto the rock whence (we) are hewn?" (Isa.51:1). Isn't it actually natural for each of us to be faithful to good? To be "perfect even as our Father" in heaven is perfect (Matt.5:48)? Haven't we been given dominion over "all the earth"—over every earthly or material tendency or weakness (Gen.1:28)? We each have the inherent capacity to be righteous. This is the fact of our being. But we have to exercise this capacity. We have to take the responsibility and make the choice to do so, regardless of the human circumstances. This is the only sure path toward health and salvation.

Our culture has become obsessed with the physical body and physical prowess. But this body is not identity, anymore than anatomy is destiny. Humanly, the body is an embodiment of thought. It is more than a biochemical organism governed by physical laws. The body can be usefully considered as a metaphor, a weathervane, an indicator of the state of our feelings, emotions, and beliefs. That's why the effort simply to treat physical symptoms or deal with physical effects is like cutting the tops off weeds. Unless the underlying fear or mental distress is dealt with, the bodily disorder will reappear.

While many admit that thoughts, feelings and emotions affect body, some question whether the reverse isn't also true: that body affects "mind." To quote Dr. Ballentine again: "The body is not merely something that is affected by the mind, but rather...the body is something that is an expression of the mind" (Dawn Magazine Vol.8, No.1, 14).

Experience, including body, is fundamentally subjective. Not circumstance, nor even one's physical identity or cultural background, as much as one's own view determines whether anything is helpful or harmful, useful or distressing. Quantum physicists today talk of "observer-created" reality, and Mary Baker Eddy concurs when she writes: "Everything is as real as you make it. What you see, feel, hear is a mode of consciousness, and can have no other reality than the sense you entertain of it" (Eddy 1887, 8).

The reality that is the transformative factor in healing is what God knows. That reality is only discerned spiritually. It is important that people come to understand themselves in terms of the spiritual qualities they express. Only thus can they progressively free themselves from equating identity with matter and existence with mortality.

Paul spoke of keeping "under" his body, and bringing it into subjection (I Cor.9:27). The best way to do that is to discipline thought by ruling out of it those negative and destructive tendencies that foster disorder, or that interfere with the body's natural immunity. Proper and moderate diet, normal exercise, cleanliness, balanced rest and purposeful activity: all these are humanly practical and wise. But the most healing attitude toward the body is to see it as "the temple of God" which is holy (I Cor.3:16-17), to care for its needs intelligently, to control it by controlling one's thinking about it, and then to forget it in serving others through witnessing to Truth.

As Jim's recovery indicates, overcoming effects of the hatred often directed at spirituality—the attack made by resentment and envy on innocence and promise—and the ensuing confusion, self-rejection, and destructive behavior may take years of maturing, but it will come. What's inevitable is that each one awaken, however gradually, to his true selfhood and spiritual heritage. This awakening enables one to express freely those God-derived qualities and talents with which he can reach out and bless others. The healthiest person is invariably the one most unselfed—most oblivious of the human personality or material ego that can suffer damage.

Memory And Forgiveness

The healing process is one of spiritual renewal, of awakening to or discovery of the spiritual selfhood that is God-created and maintained. This process necessitates uncovering or exposing the hidden inner rot, the moral decay, that eats away at individuals and at society as a whole. Making merely surface repairs to a structure that isn't basically sound will never suffice.

Awareness of the errors to be corrected makes regeneration possible. To repress, conceal, ignore, excuse, or even condone abusiveness, oppression, or victimization is to contribute to their perpetuation and works against healing. Still, as some psychologists have warned, and as some court cases have shown, the whole area of repressed memories is clouded with controversy (Loftus and Ketcham, 1995).

The much-publicized Ramona case in Napa, California, in which a father sued his daughter's psychiatrists and the Western Medical Center of Anaheim for $8 million, accusing them of implanting in her false memories of sexual abuse, resulted in an award of $475,000 to the father and an ambiguous verdict.

Writing about the case in the Los Angeles Times Magazine, Katy Butler concludes: "Those who watched the trial unfold wanted absolutes. (They wanted to) prove that child abuse is always, or never, an illusion; that victims should always, or never, be believed; that memories are always false if they're not clear or always true if they're bad enough; that the legal system can persuade a family at war to see the same truth again. In the end, it proved none of those things." ("A House Divided," 26 June, 1994, 38).

Ms. Butler points out that advocates on both sides of the issue of repressed memory concede that "memory is not a pristine videotape but subject to distortion from suggestion, trauma, and normal forgetting." Both sides admit to the possibility of true memories with false details and false memories with true details.

Much remains unknown even to neuroscientists about the mechanisms of memory. In practice, it is plain that not all repressed memories are either objectively false or true. However, it is certain that they exist and are a determinative factor in the development of coping behaviors with which some individuals struggle.

From a strictly human standpoint, most individuals who have suffered innocently may no more be able to account for what happened to them than the Ramona daughter. Personal stories are a source of truth for the individuals that tell them, and they have a right to be heard. Those who feel themselves victims have an essential need to be helped to put their stories in perspective, to mature beyond them, and finally, to move on from the past.

Here is another perspective regarding memory. It is implicit in a testimony that appeared in the Christian Science Journal by a young woman who, from early childhood through her late teens, was involved in an incestuous relationship with her father. Her mother never knew about this desecration. At the time the daughter was contemplating either running away from home or committing suicide, she enrolled in a Christian Science Sunday School.

This young woman was helped to feel the all-encompassing embrace of divine Love. Her anger, loneliness, confusion, and self-contempt began to abate. Soon thereafter, the abuse stopped. Nevertheless, she writes: "In the ensuing years I tried to erase the unpleasant memories of my childhood. But despite my efforts, I still felt a victim of my past." In a conversation with a spiritual teacher to whom she had applied for an adult class, she tearfully admitted the abuse and her struggle with feeling unworthy and unclean.

She explains: "The teacher lovingly spoke to me of my real, spiritual selfhood, which had never been touched. I remember...feeling a great sense of relief and acceptance—at last. My intuitive sense that God unconditionally loved me as His pure and perfect child was really the truth. (I realized) that, in reality, I had always been in the kingdom of Spirit, God, and that I had never had any other consciousness or memory but that of good."

She concludes: "The growing awareness of my spiritual identity is a day-to-day unfoldment, but I rejoice to know that the belief of a mortal past is but a fabrication of (the human) mind. No matter how real evil seems, it never taints man's nature as the beloved child of God. By steadily leaving behind belief in a life separate from God, I have been blessed by a sense of peace and a very harmonious marriage and family life" (November, 1985, 700-702).

Whether or not to confront a perpetrator, whether or not to pursue any means of redress, whether or not to disclose the kinds of memories that can lead to accusation and counter-accusation and can fragment families, are decisions only the individual who has suffered can make. Ultimately, however, every one must move on from the past. To be able to move on stronger, wiser, "healed," and able to help others is an attainable goal.

And, often, this requires forgiveness. One whose first forty-five years were fraught with tragedy, betrayal, disabling illness, grief, loss, regret, and sometimes despair, reached this conclusion: "It is well to know...that our material, mortal history is but the record of dreams, not of man's real existence... The heavenly intent of earth's shadows is to chasten the affections, to rebuke human consciousness and turn it gladly from a material, false sense of life and happiness, to spiritual joy and true estimate of being." She concludes: "Mere historic incidents and personal events are frivolous...unless they illustrate the ethics of Truth... The human history needs to be revised, and the material record expunged" (Eddy 1891, 21-22).

Mrs. Eddy advocates uncovering of concealment and pretense. She writes: "Though error hides behind a lie and excuses guilt, error cannot forever be concealed. Truth...unveils error... Even the disposition to excuse guilt or to conceal it is punished... Sin will receive its full penalty, both for what it is and for what it does" (Eddy 1906, 542).

This rectification comes in God's time and way, and not always here and now. Can any but God forgive sins? Jesus was challenged by the scribes on that very point (Matt.9:2-6). His healing of the paralyzed man made plain that forgiveness and healing are inseparable, and that Christliness has the power to facilitate this process for others. It is always some glimpse of divine Love's unconditionality that frees.

How do we forgive what seems unforgivable? We forgive by separating sin from the individual who commits it and by seeing sin as no part of ultimate reality—by recognizing that the offense has never gone on in the Kingdom of Heaven and remains powerless to harm or destroy God's work.

If "God requires the past" as the Bible says (Eccl.3:15), then shouldn't we turn loose of it and trust Love's recompense? To dwell on injustices, to continue to mourn what might have been, and to let resentment, anger, and bitterness fester in thought, is to remain a prisoner of the past. It also gives the past a power it doesn't deserve, and robs one's self of ever-new possibilities for present growth or gain. Moreover, lack of forgiveness is a poison in the soul, a denial of the redeeming power of divine Grace. It darkens one's own spirituality and capacity to bless.

It often seems harder to forgive one's self for past mistakes and to be free of corrosive regret and self-condemnation than to forgive another. God pardons our mistakes when they are forsaken, so shouldn't we do the same? "I have blotted out, as a thick cloud, thy transgressions, and, as a cloud, thy sins: return unto me; for I have redeemed thee" (Isa.44:22). We earn such divine mercy in the measure of our forgiveness of others' transgressions.

We can't "make a graven image" of wrongs and hurts by continually re-hashing and re-playing old memories, by allowing past ugliness to be indelibly fixed in thought. We aren't open to what is new, progressive, and healthy, until we let go of what is old and unhealthy. Ultimately, whatever evil claims it has done, it hasn't, since life is more than mortal, and earthly events are merely learning-experiences which, if we profit from, we won't have to repeat.

We don't try to account for the events in a dream, nor do we re-hash the dream and puzzle or grieve over it. Instead, we wake up and realize that it has never touched us or our loved ones and is powerless to affect what is eternally real.

Jesus taught: "Blessed are they that mourn (are grieved over evil): for they shall be comforted" (Matt.5:4). Comfort comes from the conviction that life and its promise are immortal, indestructible, and that evil of every sort is ultimately self-annihilating. Anguish over lost hopes, lost years, wasted efforts, keen disappointments gives way before the certainty that God's purpose is always fulfilled, and that no one can ever be separated from divine Love.

A primary function of the Christ is to "bind up the brokenhearted...to give beauty for ashes, the oil of joy for mourning, the garment of praise for the spirit of heaviness" (Isa.61:1-3). Moreover, Love's presence fills every void. Ultimately, whatever seems lost humanly is restored. Jesus' promises to his disciples: "I will see you again..." (John 16:22), and "lo, I am with you always..." (Matt.28:22) should undergird our conviction that we will see again those we dearly love, and that neither we nor they can be bereft of our divine Comforter, its guidance, provision, and protection. Spiritual identity and its purpose remain forever intact.

Role Of The Practitioner Or Spiritual Guide

If the human history is a dream or metaphor and not the ultimate reality, then what's important is that we learn lessons from this dream, journey on safely through it, and ultimately awaken from it. Everyone has the capacity to make this journey, and at least begin to change his or her perspectives. Sometimes others can forward the change or point the way on the journey.

Any practitioner or guide or messenger is merely an instrument, a transparency, through which the divine Spirit and its healing energy is manifest. There really is no "personal" healer. Mary Baker Eddy, who had an astonishing record of facilitating healing for others, said this: "That individual is the best healer who asserts himself the least, and thus becomes a transparency for the divine Mind, who is the only physician; the divine Mind is the scientific healer" (1896, 59).

Even Jesus rebuked the one who called him "Good Master," declaring: "...there is none good but one, that is, God" (Mark 10:17-18). The practitioner's biggest need is simply to get self, or a personal sense of responsibility as well as a personal ego, out of the way. Otherwise there is the ever-present danger of personal dependence on and even personal idolatry of the helper. The one who surrenders wholly to God's will, who establishes an individual relationship to divine Love and feels Love's presence and power, will have accomplished, at least to some degree, the move from "loneliness to solitude"—from personal success or failure to at-one-ment with an unfailing divine Good— that Nouwen describes so helpfully in Reaching Out (1975, 23-26). Then he or she will be a God-anointed guide.

Morton Kelsey describes the role of the "Christian Shaman" this way: (The one who seeks) "to guide others on a spiritual journey must (first) have undertaken his own journey. (He must be able) to bring the people to whom he ministers into context with the spiritual reality which our culture usually denies" (Kelsey 1981, 219).

It is of great importance that a counselor, practitioner, or "spiritual friend" have experienced "a movement from despair to grace," be free of outlining how resolution or healing should take place, have "gotten through (any) Messianism," and be "in full communion with his own humanity," as Tilden Edwards points out.

I agree with Edwards that one will never be able to give to others what one does not already possess and that the primary qualifications for serving as a spiritual guide relate not so much to accumulated skills but to the "self-stripping of illusion and sin that frees us to be ever more transparent and truly present" to another (Edwards 1980, 127-129). In other words, it's what we <u>are</u> more than what we do or say that is of greatest helpfulness to others.

This concept of a spiritual guide resonates well with the Bowenian view of the therapist as one who is focused "primarily on his or her own differentiation—providing vision, defining self, working at being a non-anxious presence, while taking care to remain connected" (Friedman 1991, 146). But the best helper is the one whose own consciousness is a clear transparency through which an ultimate reality can be glimpsed. We can illustrate for others only what we have, at least in some measure, glimpsed and demonstrated for ourselves.

My experience in practice confirms that one doesn't change others. People make a choice or decision to change themselves or else they respond to a transforming Grace or Love. But one can abet that choice and encourage the process, can model and support change by helping to remove resistance to it, and can assist in the re-visioning and re-framing of memories or attitudes that keep one rutted in the past or in non-progressive patterns of feeling or behavior. One can bring the alterative Truth to bear on some error or misunderstanding.

This Truth frees. The ultimate goal for each of us is to know Truth and so be released from bondage to untruth, from imprisoning self-deception and its limitations. This divine Truth is more than simply a valid human fact or truth. It is spiritual reality that transcends and has irresistible power to transform any distorted human perspective.

In a sense, we create our own realities. From a human
standpoint, this is understandable, even if self-defeating.
Hence our need for something beyond ourselves to help break
the mesmerism or hold of "false gods." The weapons that
are mighty "to the pulling down of strong holds, casting down
imaginations...and bringing into captivity every thought to
the obedience of Christ" are altogether spiritual, not carnal
or material (II Cor.10:3-5).

Are there failures in practice? Do those who would
help fall short of what they hope to achieve? Of course. I
know of no methods that can be held to a one-hundred
percent success rate. But prayer itself never fails. If we think
it does, then we've probably been praying amiss. I agree
with Krister Stendahl, former Dean of Harvard Divinity
School, as quoted in the <u>Christian Science Sentinel</u>, that
prayer isn't a means by which one achieves things. Rather, it
is a drawing closer to the ultimate Reality or divine Source
from which all things proceed (6 May, 1991, 3-7).

I also agree absolutely with Cloé Madanes that: "No
one is incurable and no situation is hopeless" (Brunner/Mazel
1991, 415-416). Not even one who is figuratively or literally
paralyzed by fear or despair is beyond the possibility of a
change of outlook or a leap of faith. Not just blind faith but
the conviction based on understanding is as important to
healing as trust is to change, but nothing is beyond the reach
of divine Grace.

What, then, can we say to one who has prayed and
still has suffered a tragic loss? We can comfort the grieving
one as we ourselves are comforted of God. We can point
out, as Robert Leslie says that "the ultimate meaning in life
is to be found...in the more-than-human world" (Leslie 1965,
119). Moral perfection is seldom attained other than

gradually, and perhaps never here. Nor is physical cure attained in every case. But the healing, transforming process goes on. We can't use God or prayer to our own ends.

Leslie further states: "Any view of life that makes any value other than God (or Ultimate Reality) absolute creates the fallacy of absolutizing what is really only relative." He continues: "It is this tendency to see all of life through the eyes of man rather than through the eyes of God that Jesus objected to so strongly" (Leslie 1965, 120).

Jesus taught: "It is not the will of your Father which is in heaven, that one of these little ones should perish" (Matt.18:14). If "it must needs be that offences come" (Matt.18:7), then let us remember that God is able to make even the "wrath of man to praise Him" (Ps.76:10)—to serve the divine purpose. Such faith begets a life of ministry rooted in an inseparable relationship to the divine.

All who seek to live such a life are engaged in healing, in creative transformation, wherever they are and whatever they're doing. They are also engaged in their own spiritual growth by responding ever more fully to the divine Love that has created all things. The writer of the First Epistle of John explained it this way: "Beloved, now are we the sons of God, and it doth not yet appear what we shall be: but we know that, when he (Christ) shall appear (when we are awakened to God's true nature and presence), we shall be like him (Christlike); for we shall see (God or Truth) as (God) is. And every man that hath this hope in him purifieth himself, even as (God) is pure" (I John 3:2-3). This is the hope and promise, the method and fulfilment, of our practice.

Servant Of God, Not Of The Problem

Too often in human efforts to be of help to others, parents, friends, teachers, support-groups, therapists, even doctors, ministers, and other practitioners can become "co-dependents," unwitting enablers to a problem rather than the resolvers of it. One can either encourage a solution, or make it more difficult.

No one can work out another's salvation, no matter how one yearns to do so. To try only inhibits another's progress and robs another of the confidence and self-esteem anyone who sees himself or herself as a victim so desperately needs. A helper can intervene strategically, as occasion demands. A helper can also model a solution, can bring to bear an alternative perspective, can be an agent of healing Grace. But if anyone repeatedly tries to spare another the consequences of wrong thoughts, acts, or behaviors, that helper will only entrench those negative patterns and inhibit progress.

Illness or incapacity—whether mental, physical, or financial—often becomes the ultimate excuse. Victimhood is an inevitable by-product of ignorance and entrenched attitudes, of unbridled self-will and unwillingness to change. In the final analysis, each of us must take responsibility for ourselves. We must each use whatever talents we have been given. We must contribute, be useful, serve, give, in order to be healthy and happy. The goal of any spiritual guide or friend must be to aid another in doing this by helping him think and act productively.

Empathy must not become sympathy. Holding another compassionately, understanding his or her needs, being present to another, while still retaining a perspective, still discerning the corrective reality, is what's needed. One can't get into a dream and then help to break it. From a spiritual standpoint, the need is to discern the specific counterfact that derives from ultimate Truth, and then trust that Truth to operate and bring about the needed adjustment humanly.

The problem is seldom if ever simply the presenting trauma but the sequence of behaviors, attitudes, perspectives that have grown from this trauma and become entrenched in an individual's thinking, thereby dominating one's experience and becoming the over-riding or determinative factor in all his or her approaches and actions. In other words, the person becomes a servant of the problem, and the problem becomes the master.

That's the idolatry that must be broken. Its hold can be quickly loosened with the in-breaking of a transformative truth, or it can sometimes take a long process of re-framing memories and perspectives, changing attitudes, correcting destructive behaviors, before one can see oneself differently and begin to recognize that there are choices.

In fact, one always has choices. The important thing is to choose intelligently, rightly, from a position of strength, not weakness, and hopefully, with some insight into the spiritual fundamentals of being. An editorial in The Christian Science Monitor entitled: "Violence and Choice" pointed out that violence is learned behavior (12 January, 1994, 22). Certainly, when more American lives are lost to violence every five years than in the entire Viet Nam war, it's time for a determined re-thinking of the effects of early abuse, of experiences that demean and embitter, of the constant barrage of violent acts in movies, TV programming and video-games, as well as the underlying lack of spiritual values that translates into a trivializing of human life and an abdication of moral responsibility.

We can't escape the fact that whatever shapes thought will shape experience. Therefore, we must always "choose whom (we) will serve" (Josh.24:15)—choose what thoughts we will entertain. Even if we don't choose and aren't responsible for negative or tragic events, we always have the ability to choose how we will view or approach them—if not as a child or in the developing years, then as an adult, when we have "put away childish things" (I Cor.13:11) or perspectives.

Then, we have the opportunity to turn challenge into blessing, stumbling-blocks into stepping-stones. In fact, the sharper the experience, the more likely it is to turn us "to the arms of divine Love," that is, to a divine source for comfort, meaning, and healing (Eddy 1906, 322).

There is never a time or circumstance when one does not have recourse to the spiritual: to the fact that the eternal Parent is God; that one can never be outside the divine Presence or separated from divine Love; that one's true being is inviolable and indestructible; and that even in the midst of some trial or trauma, an alternative reality that has the power to guide, protect, uplift, transform can be glimpsed. Ultimately, nothing has the power to harm or destroy God's work which is eternally and spiritually perfect. God doesn't form deformity, either moral or physical. Apparent human imperfection can neither alter that fact, nor forever obscure it.

What I say to anyone struggling with some "dark night of the soul," some hidden or painfully clear inner anguish, some unrelieved torment or unresolved problem, is this: Refuse to allow any tragic experience to dominate your thought, discolor your outlook, or fester within you. Choose instead to turn from it, and dwell with what is spiritually real. That doesn't mean concealing, excusing, or pretending about the wrong, only refusing to give it power over you. Refuse to react with either fear, anger, or revenge, or to give in either to self-pity or self-condemnation. Blaming and retaliation only perpetuate the harm.

When needed, tell the truth by exposing the evil, and pray for the wisdom and courage to do this in a way that will be constructive and healing. Evil wants concealment. It threatens penalties for exposure, but the greatest penalty of all comes from allowing it to become a god and to dominate your thoughts and acts, thus robbing you of your true individuality. Everyone's birthright is freedom and dominion, and you can claim it. You can always exercise your innate ability to think rightly, to forgive, to love, to bless. Your health and happiness depend on this.

You can pray, reaching out with all your heart to that Higher Power that is always with you. You can ask to be shown what the fundamental Truth is and how best to bear It witness. You can trust God's ability to "make all things new" (Rev.21:5) and to overturn whatever isn't right. Divine Love will heal you of your wounds and restore whatever has seemed lost to you.

I have proved for myself, and so have countless others, that God gives "fresh opportunities every hour" (Eddy 1906, 19). We can't forever be deprived of what God gives, nor can our labors be wasted. There is never a dead-end, never a time or a situation where there can't be growth and renewal. Often that renewal comes when one can use one's own trauma and the lessons learned from it to help others. Great rewards come from attempts to ameliorate others' suffering, from involvement in practical and effective efforts to meet others' needs, and from participating in others' healings.

If you seem to be a victim of circumstances over which you have no control, know that you can always control the feelings and thoughts you entertain about them. A spiritual approach to healing recognizes that everyone has a responsibility, not for abusive circumstances, but for his own approach to dealing with them. Each of us always has a choice. We can use the misfortune as a perpetual excuse for not achieving or contributing or else for striking out at others in retaliation. Or we can recognize that others also have needs, and that everyone has obligations to respond in love to the One that has created and sustains us all.

No one has just to react and be at the mercy of devastating emotions and the ills they produce. Nothing can take away the grace, mercy, joy, and peace that come from individual at-one-ment with our common divine Source. Even if you've been going in the wrong direction for a long time, you can at once turn around. Nothing can keep you from returning to your spiritual roots, your original innocence, nor can anything lock you into a hopeless mental or physical state. You can refuse to allow the poisons of shock, grief, bitterness, rage, resentment, hatred, helplessness, complaint, resignation, to abide in your thought. You can, instead, "make you a new heart and a new spirit" (Ezek.18:31). You can focus on what is everlastingly real, good, and beautiful, and be grateful for it. You can know that what God appoints can't be disappointed. Only the divine purpose can be fulfilled in you.

What you learn from any difficult experience is gain to you. It can make you stronger, less self-entwined, more humble, more compassionate of others. When you pass through some wilderness, and grow spiritually because of it, then you serve and honor God and not the problem. Moreover, when you find the lesson or blessing in any suffering, you overcome it and are ready to be done with it. That's what it means to be "lifted up from the earth" (John 12:32). Such spiritual altitude gives you vision and dominion; it lifts you beyond the reach of heart-break and despair and draws to you those you can bless.

Chapter Four

INDIVIDUAL CASE HISTORIES

"ye are my witnesses...that I am God" (Isa.43:12)

Most people are aware of significant Biblical and historical examples of redemption from bondage, of healing, vindication, and restoration through grace and forgiveness. But there are also many present day examples. All of the following experiences are ones with which I have personal knowledge or have had professional involvement. They are presented with the recognition that each individual's story is unique, and that needed change or awakening can come in a variety of ways. They are also illustrations of a disturbed human sense of things conforming to what is spiritually real—of divine reality embracing and transforming the human. Hopefully, these few, but wide-ranging accounts can point to what is possible for all those who, for whatever reason, feel themselves victims.

There are commonalities to each account. Often there was a choice or decision, sometimes attained through suffering, to stop being a victim by no longer allowing the past to dominate present possibilities. That choice involved a readiness to stop using the past or some circumstance as an excuse and to start taking responsibility for one's thoughts and acts. There was also a shared determination to grow spiritually both by arriving at a better understanding of one's self in relation to one's Maker and by confronting the "demons" of fear, resentment, shame, guilt, and anger.

Ultimately, the individuals whose stories these are came to regard their own pain and the lessons learned from conquering that pain as a means of being helpful to others—of making a positive and meaningful contribution to others' healing.

There was recognition in these cases of the need to make changes and a willingness to do so, preceded by an unwillingness to accept the verdict of "incurability." Various aspects of incurability, such as the notion that change for the better was impossible; that some problem was simply unsolvable—there was "no way out;" that an affliction was so extreme nothing could be done, or some attitudes or behaviors so ingrained they could never be altered, were repudiated. Personality "types" were not regarded as either definitive or determinative. Nor was anyone seen as locked into patterns of self-defeating behavior. Rather, freedom came as each one in his or her own way established and accepted fundamental spiritual truths relevant to true individuality and its inviolability.

It is important to recognize that addictions, compulsive behaviors, obsessive living in the past, destructive "acting-out," either self-gratification and self-indulgence, or self-punishment and self-condemnation, can't be resolved through human will because they are manifestations of such will. They are indications of a self-asserting human ego and a spiritually immature perspective that must ultimately become cognizant of and yield to the divine Will or Law.

One opposite of willfulness is willingness—the willingness to seek, yield to, trust, and comply with God's law and thus benefit from its operation. Such yielding involves humility, or the recognition that genuine selfhood remains inseparable from God—from the eternal Soul, Mind, or Life which we each individually express and which we must ultimately honor.

Childhood Sexual Abuse And Its Consequences

Scott and Randy, now in their late 30's, each suffered extended sexual abuse within their separate families as children. Scott is the oldest of three boys. His mother divorced when he was just into his teens, and he spent several years living with his brothers, mother, and step-father in a situation that was abnormal and extremely harmful, not only for Scott, but for his younger brothers as well. The step-father, a man of no religious convictions, molested all the boys. As a result, and despite his early upbringing in Christian Science, Scott began drinking. Happily, he was lifted out of the situation when he was sent to boarding school and then to college, where his experience was more normal.

But he found himself unable to relate easily to girls and eventually concluded that he was homosexual. This orientation, and the encounters that followed, together with accelerating alcoholism, were extremely upsetting to Scott, and he entered therapy to find help.

Randy, by contrast, was abused very early (at ages 4 and 5) by older boys, and then describes himself as "an object of (sexual) experimentation" and bullying from ages 13-15 by friends of his older brother. He is the middle child of three boys and was never close to either brother. He was musically talented, while they were sports-minded. The father, who was a high-school teacher and coach, took little interest in his own sons, and was unfaithful to their mother. Randy's dad left the family suddenly when Randy was in college, and he had to drop out in his sophomore year to help the family. What he describes as "an unhealthy attachment or dependence" between himself and his mother then developed.

Randy has also struggled with sexual orientation, but more with a sense of abandonment by his father and subsequent emotional and financial deprivation. He went through a difficult period of joblessness, but is now employed and endeavoring to start anew.

Over a period of months, I was privileged to work with both young men and to see significant transformation in their perspectives. This has resulted in progress in their experiences in many ways—in their work situations, in their ability to relate in a healthier way to others, and in their self-acceptance and esteem. Scott was able to stop drinking and has renewed interest in his own spiritual growth. Though his path hasn't been smooth, he has developed several satisfying friendships with young women, and has been able to contribute in creative ways to others.

Both young men had experienced (and struggled against) an unnatural enmeshment with their mothers, which was compounded by pity and a false sense of responsibility. Both also felt a deep yearning for a father's attention and affirmation. I feel it was this yearning, as well as confusion resulting from the earlier abuse, that led to homosexual encounters.

They both were interested to learn that psychologists believe sexual performance becomes far more important to personality development for men than for women. Early sexual abuse often calls into question a boy's entire sense of male identity and self-worth (McCarthy and McCarthy 1993, 95-97)

But the most transformative truth for both Scott and Randy has been that true identity is fundamentally spiritual, not physical, and that it is each one's relationship to God that is determinative, not only of identity (including gender identity) but of worth, wholeness, character, place, purpose. It also became plain to them that, in a culture that has become obsessed with body, physical appearance, and sensuality, there is an absolute need to identify one's self in terms of spiritual qualities: to free identity from heredity, from time or material circumstance, and from a human past or history.

This practical counsel was comforting to them both: "From a human standpoint of good, mortals must first choose between evils, and of two evils choose the less... Wisdom in human action begins with what is nearest right under the circumstances, and thence achieves the absolute" (Eddy 1896, 288-289). They began to see that they could make choices, and that past circumstances could not lock them into self-defeating attitudes or behaviors.

They also glimpsed to an extent that not material success nor sexual satisfaction but the shedding of a limited and false sense of self ("the old man with his deeds") is the ultimate aim and reward of the human journey. Achievement of the freedom and dominion of their true identity as children of God ("the new man...renewed...after the image of Him that created him," Col.3: 9-10) has become their fundamental goal.

Randy wrote me: "I have learned about forgiveness and the redemption of the past and have learned to focus on my indestructible and inseparable relationship to God, the only true Father-Mother...from whom can come only good. I have begun to see my self-worth and to acknowledge and claim my innocence. I have, to some degree, routed out the 'ghosts' of the past and have begun to let natural abilities and talents...unfold and be expressed for God's own purpose, (and to feel) complete, fruitful, satisfied."

When despair gives way to hope and fear to courage, when one glimpses more of his genuine selfhood and lives more in accord with it, there is a progressive freeing from bondage to past hurts and also an enhanced spirituality. The innate ability to connect in an affirmative and healing way with others and with God develops. Then one experiences divine Grace and its power to "make all things new" (Rev. 21:5), to wash all things clean.

Physical Abuse

Myrtle Smyth is a Christian Science Practitioner and Lecturer from Belfast, Northern Ireland. Mrs. Smyth has written and spoken widely about her own experience of domestic violence, which included homelessness, poverty, fear, shame, child abuse, and ultimately, divorce.

In a talk entitled, "Neither Villains nor Victims," she cites statistics that indicate between three and four million women in the United States suffer physical abuse each year. In the United States, domestic violence accounts for more injuries to women than mugging, auto accidents, and rape combined. Nevertheless, until very recently there has been a conspiracy of silence with regard to this severe problem— an almost universal attitude of neglect and compromise.

Mrs. Smyth suffered such violence for 30 years— starting on the second day of her marriage to a member of the Merchant Marine. In fact, as a child she had often been beaten by her mother, and had eagerly seized the opportunity to marry and have a home of her own. As is so often the case, it was a move "out of the frying pan and into the fire." In the early years of her marriage, when living in foreign countries, she struggled with isolation, self-doubt, shame, and fear.

Once, when her oldest boy was five and the family lived in Malta, her husband beat the little boy unconscious, and the child was taken to a hospital. Myrtle resolved then to do everything possible to spare her children, even at the cost of her own life. She mothered five children. The sixth was stillborn due to beatings she suffered during that pregnancy.

After the family settled in Belfast, police were often called to their home to quell the husband's violence, until a voluminous file of incidents built up in the police files. In spite of this, little corrective action was taken by the authorities. When she finally decided to leave and told her husband so, he threw her and the four children then still at home out in the snow, with nothing but the clothes on their backs. She spent several nights in a shelter for battered women until friends from church helped locate a place for them to live. Time and again, the husband would track them down, break his way in and literally destroy the simple home they had made. Over a four year period, she had to move eight times. The husband even quit his job so he wouldn't have to pay them anything.

Once he broke into the home while she and the children were at church, and again when another child was visiting. On that occasion, he literally pulled a washing machine loaded with clothes out of the wall. A neighbor saw what was happening and called the police, and it took ten policemen to subdue him and take him away.

Because of daily violence connected with the political situation in Belfast, as well as frequent violence within the home, Myrtle wondered whether she could ever be free of scars, including the tormenting fears and haunting memories. By this time, she had become an earnest student of Christian Science and a practitioner of its teachings. It was this effort to help others, she feels, that was her own salvation.

She began to see herself, and others, not as victims of circumstances, but as children of God. Isaiah, Chapter 54, was her constant companion, as well as an article entitled, "Love Your Enemies." There it states: "Simply count your enemy to be that which defiles, defaces, and dethrones the Christ-image that you should reflect. Whatever purifies, sanctifies, and consecrates human life, is not an enemy, however much we suffer in the process." The article continues: "We have no enemies. Whatever envy, hatred, revenge—the most remorseless motives that govern mortal mind—whatever these try to do, shall 'work together for good to them that love God'" (Eddy 1896, 8-13).

Myrtle became stronger, more courageous, more compassionate of others, even of her husband, who had been abused as a child and who had a recurrent alcohol problem. At the time she went through the divorce—a difficult process in Northern Ireland—she was able to pray for her husband. Her freedom came, she claims, not from the divorce, but from being able to forgive.

Supply came to the family, sometimes in unexpected ways. The four younger children were able to attend a boarding school in England. Loneliness was overcome, and much broader opportunities for service to others opened up for Myrtle, including work as a prison chaplain to Northern

Ireland terrorists, several of whom experienced remarkable healings as a result of her prayers.

In an article entitled: "The time for forgiveness has arrived," Myrtle writes: "The only thinking we have to change is ours. We are not responsible for the thoughts of other people. But by forgiving them and separating the sin from the sinner...we are acknowledging the genuine spiritual identity of the person, and this can help bring healing." She continues: "It's interesting that part of a definition of the word condemn...is 'to pronounce incurable.' To believe that any person is incurable is to believe that there's some condition or individual beyond God's help..."

She points out that the husband she thought was such an enemy turned her more and more to God to find her answers until she learned to depend upon God alone. "This," she says, "gave me a freedom that I had never known before: a sense of absolute completeness and wholeness. And it provided such living proofs of God's loving care that I could never doubt (God) again."

She concludes: "Only divine Love will heal this world. Retaliation and all the bombs and missiles and ammunition in arsenals around the globe can never heal. Neither can all the human arguments and reasoning from a...material basis... Regardless of how you have been wronged or abused, your forgiveness will surely have its healing effect" (Smyth 1993, 15-17).

Accidental Injury And Harm

The law of God is not random; there is no element of chance, of unpredictability, partiality, or irregularity in its operation. It isn't casual, occasional, accidental, coincidental, sporadic, unplanned, or ineffective. How, then, do we account for accidents or even natural disasters? I suggest accidents can be seen as the product of human belief and expectation, sometimes of carelessness and unalertness, or even of deliberate malice. While no individuals are "accident-prone," what appear as accidental occurrences can result from unhealed errors in thought, and they can compel, although sometimes at great cost, needed spiritual growth.

It should be plain that general acceptance of random good fortune leaves one's mental door open to misfortune. The tremendous surge of legalized gambling as entertainment, together with advertising sweepstakes that utilize luck and chance commercially to promote products, exert a pervasive and unhealthy cultural influence with regard to safety.

Not all the safety features that can be devised—though I heartily commend the heightened responsibility for product safety shown by many companies today—can save an individual from his own or another's undoing. But God can. Indeed, even in the midst of the most widespread disasters, such as Hurricane Andrew in Florida in the fall of 1992, or the February, 1993 earthquake in southern California, individuals who appeal to God's law have experienced the blessing and protection of that law.

One incident reported on ABC and NBC news the morning after a firestorm which swept through the community of Laguna Beach, California on October 27, 1994 was that of the preservation of the Ingwerson family home. Among many newspaper accounts, one reported the following: "It began a few hours after an arsonist's torch set off a fire storm that seared southern California...Lona Ingwerson (together with her daughter and granddaughter) evacuated their oceanside home in Laguna Beach...Tom Hobbs, the Orange County fire fighter working at the command post yesterday said to the newspaper, 'This fire blazed with such intensity traveling at 100 miles an hour that I cannot discount the force of divine intervention in the case of their home.' "

When the family re-entered the home the following day, they found everything intact, nothing damaged or even blackened, in the midst of an entire hillside of devastation. The telephone was ringing with a call from Munich, Germany. The caller revealed that church members there had been praying for the Ingwerson's protection. Repeated calls with similar messages came from other locations around the world—a consequence of Mrs. Ingwerson's lecturing in many of these places during several preceding years, and members of her audiences knowing where she lived and how to reach her.

During the night when everything had seemed lost, Mrs. Ingwerson said she kept remembering these lines from a hymn in the Christian Science hymnal: "When through fiery trials thy pathway shall lie, My grace, all sufficient, shall be thy supply; The flame shall not hurt thee; I only design Thy dross to consume and thy gold to refine" (Hymn 123 from "K" in Rippon's selection 1787).

In an unpublished talk given in 1994 at Daystar in Fort Lauderdale, Florida about the experience, Mrs. Ingwerson added this: "I wish everyone's home had been saved. But I'll tell you what else I wish. I wish that everyone relied on God in emergencies (and) in little ways as well... I don't feel I have to justify answered prayer... How would I feel if our house had burned in the fire? Grateful that our

<u>home</u> hadn't. Grateful to have a non-combustible home in a world of very combustible houses."

She concluded: "You may feel that you haven't been through a fiery trial and come out victorious as yet. Can you trust that you will? Can you trust that God loves you too much to let you down; that this is a time of renewal and not retreat?... (God's) not going to let you down. Think about the little trials. You know the trust that takes us through the big fires is the one that starts with the little matches we put out before the fire ever gets started... There is such a thing as a spiritual commitment, a spiritual priority which we need to establish in our lives and our homes not just when we have nothing else to do but maybe when we have everything else to do; not just when we have an emergency but maybe when everything looks great. We make it a priority in our lives so that when we do have a need we can turn to God, fearless and unafraid."

The recognition of God's presence and power can bring needed guidance and protection in the face of severe trials, or it can erase the effects of such trials, even long after they occur. Such was the experience of a New York City policeman who suffered a line-of-duty injury that left him crippled for over 12 years. Despite the finest hospital, surgical, and rehabilitative treatment provided over a three year period, orthopedic surgeons advised John Ondrak that he would be permanently crippled. Because of the disablement, he was examined by a police review board and was retired from the department.

The doctors reported that the bones in John's feet had calcified into nearly solid pieces, severely limiting their flexibility and motion. Though he eventually learned to walk laboriously assisted by two canes, he struggled with constant pain. Even with daily sedatives, sleep was difficult and getting out of bed an ordeal.

In his personal account reprinted from The Christian Science Journal of September, 1982, he tells of reaching a point where he seriously considered suicide. He had been an athlete all his life, and now he was filled with anger and resentment against the tragedy that had put an end to his career and his health.

His wife, a life-long Christian Scientist, had encouraged his study of the Christian Science textbook, but he had considered himself an atheist and his thinking incompatible with its teachings. However, at this extremity he opened Science and Health and was filled with a sense of peace. He writes: "Now was the time to lean on something much greater than material means and human will."

In his search for the truth concerning God and creation, he became so preoccupied with study of the Bible and the Christian Science textbook that he never knew exactly when his healing came. One morning, he was overjoyed to realize that there was no more pain, and that the tragic episode of invalidism was over. He writes: "...when I put personal self aside and did search honestly and diligently, the truth that makes all men free came alive for me, as it will for anyone who earnestly seeks... This former police officer, who had been told he might never walk again, now runs three or four miles each day. As I begin my daily run, I thank God for His love, for His power and presence, and pray that I be guided to do whatever will bring glory to His name."

In her verification of her husband's testimony, Mrs. Ondrak mentions that when she was called to the hospital at the time of the accident, she was asked to sign a consent form that included the words: "Permission to amputate." She told the doctor that she could not consent to any such operation. She concludes: "To see my husband again run, bicycle, dance, and walk without a limp or defect of any kind after so many years of agonizing disability, has indeed proved to me that 'with God all things are possible'" (Peel 1987, 64-68).

Another experience which proves the transformative power of Truth, occurred many years ago when our family went to Colorado for a ski week. Accompanying us was Diane, a young woman who was a graduate student and an expert skier. She came especially to help with our three young children.

We were traversing a gentle slope where the snow was deep—not packed down. Diane caught a ski tip in the heavy snow and went down, but her ski binding didn't release. We returned to help her when she clearly couldn't get up. She had a moment's discomfort when we had to turn the foot and take off the ski and boot.

During the trip down the mountain on a stretcher, Diane was not uncomfortable. Her decision was to be taken to the clinic for X-rays. The clinic was full when we arrived, and Diane was obviously calm and free of pain, so we waited quite a while for others to be cared for first.

Finally Diane was rather nonchalantly taken in for X-rays by a young intern, but when he came out with the prints sometime later his face was white with concern. The pictures showed two breaks, one quite severe. In removing her ski trousers, the bones had been moved radically out of position, and the doctors then proceeded to attempt to set them back in place. Only then, and with the weight of apprehension in their thought resting on her, did Diane experience pain but she refused any medication. Three separate attempts were made to set the bones but without success. Finally the doctors left on the third cast which went from the foot up her leg to the thigh and said she must remain overnight for observation. They were urging a trip into Denver the next day for surgery and pinning of the bones and predicted many dire results if this were not done.

I remained with Diane praying earnestly, and she slept peacefully through the night. In the morning, she chose to leave the clinic, refusing any further medical help. Her progress the next three days was remarkable, and she flew home to resume work on a graduate degree, using crutches. She had the cast removed in less than a month and was able to walk, which the doctors had predicted she might never do. There was however an abnormalcy.

One leg seemed a bit shorter than the other with a visible deformity in the shin area. Gradually, over several years, these problems also disappeared. Diane was able to complete her studies without hindrance, and today leads an extremely active life. I couldn't tell which leg was involved. More important than this outcome however, was the adjusting and straightening out of thought that took place. Not long before our ski trip, Diane had made a break with a young man of whom she was fond, but whose values and life style she felt to be incompatible with her own. A few years before that, her mother had passed on, and her dad had quickly remarried—a situation which left her feeling unsupported and very crippled in her affections. It was as if the pins had been knocked out from under her, and the mental anguish she was feeling was, at times, very acute.

Diane's need was to look to her unbroken relationship with her divine Source, her eternal parent and best friend. She saw that joy, support, and a sense of being cherished came from God, not from person, and could never be lost. As her relationship with her father and new step-mother mended and normalized, so did the bones in her leg. Eventually, she found herself walking "with Love along the way," and feeling "the joy that none can take away," as Hymn 139 in the Christian Science Hymnal says.

What was required in this case was an art beyond any surgeon's skill—the repair and re-ordering of thought, the bringing of thought into alignment with Truth and Love, so that her unbroken perfection, her spiritual wholeness, could appear. If God's creation, made in the divine image, weren't whole, complete, intact, immune to harm, none of us could hope to demonstrate that fact humanly. But because wholeness is the spiritual fact, we can and must prove it, at least to some degree, here and now.

Diseases Diagnosed Incurable Or Fatal

God does not afflict. What has been interpreted historically in Biblical or theological terms to imply God's wrath or punishment simply refers to the inevitable self-punishment of mistaken or disturbed thinking. In James we read: "...God cannot be tempted with evil, neither tempteth he any man; But every man is tempted, when he is drawn away of his own lust, and enticed" (1:13-14).

Moreover, the Bible is full of promises of God's mercy and forgiveness. Coupled with the injunction: "...return unto the Lord thy God; for thou hast fallen by thine iniquity," is the assurance: "I will heal their backsliding, I will love them freely" (Hosea 14:1,4). Again in Isaiah: "I have blotted out, as a thick cloud, thy transgressions, and, as

a cloud, thy sins: return unto me; for I have redeemed thee"
(44:22).

Throughout the Bible are assurances of the divine
intent to save, to heal, restore, repair, renew. The Psalmist
sang: "...thou hast delivered my soul from death, mine eyes
from tears, and my feet from falling" (Ps. 116:8). And again:
"Bless the Lord, O my soul, and forget not all his benefits:
Who forgiveth all thine iniquities; who healeth all thy
diseases; Who redeemeth thy life from destruction..."
(Ps.103:2-4).

Today many people who struggle with illness and
incapacity, with medical verdicts of hopelessness and
incurability, are turning to the Great Physician as an unfailing
divine Source for health and wholeness. This turning is from
the standpoint of acknowledging God's goodness and
conforming thoughts and lives to that goodness, and is with
reverence and humility but not from a posture of pleading.

It is the Spirit of God—of Truth, Life, and Love,
that heals. In answer to the question: "Is it wrong to pray for
the recovery of the sick?" Mrs. Eddy replies: "Not if we
pray...with the understanding that God has given all things
to those who love Him; but pleading with infinite Love to
love us, or to restore health and harmony, and then to admit
that it has been lost under His government, is the prayer of
doubt and mortal belief that is unavailing in divine Science"
(Eddy 1896, 59).

The word, science, according to Webster implies
"systematized knowledge formulated with reference to the
discovery of general truths or the operation of general laws."
The science of Christianity, then, embodies demonstrable
or provable knowledge based upon the fundamental
principles taught by Christ Jesus. It is a practical salvation—

not in some far off heaven, but here and now within all those who conform their thoughts and lives to these principles.

Healing or redemption is the repeatable, expectable effect of such scientific Christianity, as promised in Jeremiah: "After those days, saith the Lord, I will put my law in their inward parts, and write it in their hearts...And they shall teach no more every man his neighbor...saying, Know the Lord: for they shall all know me, from the least of them unto the greatest of them..." (31: 33-34).

Spiritual healing is not miraculous or mysterious, but is the effect of God understood. It occurs as fear, ignorance of God, and sin or mistaken thinking and wrong doing are corrected and replaced with Truth or cast out. Spiritual healing results not from the pursuit of physical well-being but from the search for spiritual wholeness: the determination to live so as to glorify God and to both glimpse and bear witness to spiritual reality.

There is no failure in this search, no discouragement or defeat in the quest for a greater understanding of ultimate Truth. Despite the severity or extent of some difficulty, nothing can alter or destroy the spiritual facts of being. Healing comes, sometimes suddenly but more often gradually, with the in-breaking of these spiritual facts into consciousness. Healing is a change of thought, and this inner change inevitably brings with it a change in body and circumstances. Thought always externalizes itself. The inner or spiritual is what determines the outward or human.

Debbie's experience is another good illustration of this point. Several years ago, she was rushed to a prominent clinic and diagnosed with chronic pancreatitis and liver disease. An award-winning young saleswoman, she had ignored earlier warnings about stress and the use of alcohol.

Her parents, who were active Christian Scientists and had given their daughter Sunday School training as a child, were informed that her condition was inoperable and terminal. She appeared near death.

In this extremity Debbie determined to transfer from the clinic to a Christian Science care facility, and treatment in Christian Science was begun. Within a fairly short time normal bodily functioning resumed and attendant problems began to abate. Then the real healing began. Here's how she describes it: "As I became again aware of my situation, I suffered a great deal of incredulity and fear. I had not been to any church in over twenty years, rarely thought about God, and had little confidence in prayer...

"One day, a Christian Science nurse asked me to make a list of everything I had to be grateful for. I looked at her and thought, 'You must be kidding.' After she left, I began to ponder why I was still alive and, right then, it came to me that although I had given up on God, He had never abandoned me. He had been with me throughout my life in many instances that I began to recall. The statement that God is All-in-all suddenly took on a new meaning, and I knew that if God had taken me this far, He would take me all the way. As I glimpsed my spiritual being for the first time, my thought about myself and my condition totally changed, and I knew I was healed."

In order to return to work, Debbie had to submit to a thorough medical examination. The doctor attested to what he described as a remarkable recovery. Not that she has had no further challenges. She has surmounted incredulity, hostility, and rivalry at work. The sudden passing of her mother, followed by the death of her husband, who was not a Christian Scientist, from cancer, left her feeling crippled emotionally, while the strong medication given her during her brief stay at the clinic resulted in a deteriorating bone condition that has made walking normally a struggle.

Christian Scientists generally approach every challenge as an opportunity. They have learned to look for and entertain the angel or blessing in every "wrathful and afflictive" circumstance (Eddy 1906, 574). The fact remains that God and His image, infinite Mind and its idea, can never be separated or alienated—other than in belief, or to a mistaken human sense of things. God is with us at all times and in every circumstance because we are the very expression of the divine Being.

Our need always is to know this and to live it in increasing measure. As we do, we come home. That is, we consciously dwell in the awareness of God's presence, where we know that we are God's beloved.

"No hate or harm, no loss or deprivation, can touch or affect one's real being—the spiritual selfhood at one with the Father... This genuine selfhood can be neither victim nor perpetrator... To glimpse, even in a degree, this spiritual fact is to experience God's presence here and now...and to be found whole, complete, secure... Nothing is of greater importance to mankind than this awakening" (Richardson 1994, 33-34).

The following experience of Eleanor's also took place several years ago. A long-time Christian Science practitioner, Eleanor began to have great difficulty moving about. The situation grew steadily worse until she was in constant pain and almost helpless—unable to dress or take care of herself. In desperation and concern for the burden she was placing on her husband, who was nearing retirement, she consented to medical diagnosis and treatment. In so doing, she withdrew from her branch church and her public practice.

She felt as if everything she held dear, every truth she loved, her very purpose in living, were threatened. The medical diagnosis was degenerative osteoarthritis with no hope of a cure. There was the possibility of radical surgery, but that would leave her crippled and helpless for the rest of her life. The pain-killing medications left her dazed and unable to think clearly—until one day she utterly rebelled at the whole sorry situation and returned to Christian Science, determined to prove it.

Together, we began to reestablish a clear understanding of the spiritual facts of being. Many fears and hurts were uncovered and dealt with, including longstanding disagreement with a fellow church member and some painful discord among family members. Eleanor began to reason from the standpoint that because God's ideas are held together in the divine law, they can only work together harmoniously.

She saw that God's children don't rub each other the wrong way: there isn't friction between them, nor can one inhibit the freedom or interfere with the right activity of another. In the deepest sense, she saw her church and her identity as God-constituted and governed, functioning perfectly, free from rigidity, malformation, or deterioration.

Improvement was steady. Within the year, her healing was complete. She and her husband were able to take a long-desired trip that included white-water rafting. In connection with her husband's retirement, they moved to a new home, where Eleanor is again active in church and in the practice of Christian Science.

I wrote about the experience: "Such a restoration evidences the grace God bestows—the exemption from penalty and entitlement to harmony and blessing inherent in being obedient to His law... Recognition that what appears to be a discordant, mistaken, suffering, desperately unhappy, disgraced, and deprived mortal isn't anyone's true nature acts to save us from believing in and being victimized by such a lie... Each of us humanly can grow in grace because we are already and eternally graced of the Father... To know this...makes us sufficient to any need... It gives us an unlabored, unfrustrated, unrestricted sense of moving in accord with God, at the impulse of His love..." (Richardson 1987, 5-7)

My husband, Bart, experienced a remarkable healing as a young man that bears out the above. He was discharged from the Navy near the end of World War II with a medical diagnosis of tuberculosis of the spine. X-rays showed decomposition of certain vertebrae. The physicians told him the condition was fatal. Even if he should survive, they said, he would never be able to walk.

Bart wrote about his experience: "At that point it mattered little to me whether I died or not if only I could understand better how the power of God operates in human experience." With a medical discharge and in a full body cast and receiving nursing care but no medical treatment, he persisted in earnestly praying and studying Christian Science. Nevertheless, about a month after leaving the hospital, he drifted into an increasingly severe fever. The body cast was cut away. Finally, he could no longer retain food or water. A Christian Science practitioner was at his bedside.

Bart's testimony continues: "As I approached what seemed to be my inevitable passing, a deep-seated guilt about a tormenting resentment poured from my lips. The practitioner's response was immediate and vigorous: 'You don't have to love a person, just express Love.' I have come to understand this as meaning that we don't have to love personal sense or human will... Divine Love engenders true human affection...

"It was as though a heavy burden had been lifted from me. A wave of relief and peace swept over me. The fever and retching ceased. And with a divine assurance...I got up and walked. The fatal aspect of the disease was ended, though the healing was not yet complete..."

Later on, Bart spent time at a Christian Science nursing facility and was put in touch with another practitioner. Together they discussed how the divine operates in human experience, how spiritual ideas are tangible and real and how the spiritual determines the outward.

Bart's testimony concludes: "Before, I had been convinced that everything I touched and saw was material and needed to be got rid of, and so it had felt hypocritical to affirm I was spiritual. But now I saw that man is spiritual here and now and that matter is nothing more than a subjective denial and obscuration of true being" (van Eck 1989, 37-39).

This was the transforming truth, and within a few weeks, he regained complete strength, flexibility and freedom in his back; the drainage from his thigh stopped, and the wound healed. In two months, he was attending college, and decades later, still runs with joy and exhibits above normal health and strength. He is convinced that God's plan and purpose must be worked out in each of us.

In <u>Science and Health</u>, Mrs. Eddy refers to disease as "an image of thought externalized." She writes that "Disease is always induced by a false sense mentally entertained, not destroyed" (Eddy 1906, 411). Health, on the other hand, "is the consciousness of the unreality of pain and disease; or, rather, the absolute consciousness of harmony and of nothing else" (Eddy 1891, 11).

Healing, then, involves awakening; it proceeds from finding out that all is well. Healing necessitates the refuting of false belief with Truth, and the conforming of human thought to divine reality. It often involves comforting those who grieve or suffer, liberating the captives of ignorance and fear, opening blind eyes and deaf ears, freeing those imprisoned by past misuse or abuse. Nothing less than spiritual transformation can make the deserts of human experience "rejoice, and blossom as the rose" (Isa.35:1).

<u>Family Strife</u>

Families today suffer terrible discord and great duress. In general, too little attention is given to the destructive effect of societal trends on families, particularly the endemic criminality and violence growing out of the pervasive drug use of our culture. Unstable economic pressures, population mobility, media influence and changing family structures, as well as the breakdown of moral values in this secular, consumer society are other obvious factors.

In the <u>Atlantic Monthly</u> article entitled: "Dan Quayle was Right," the author states: "Research shows that many children from disrupted families have a harder time achieving intimacy in a relationship, forming a stable marriage, or even holding a steady job" (Whitehead 1993, 35). This hardly bodes well for a coming generation, less than half of which will live continuously with their biological parents throughout childhood.

Certainly, no individual exists in isolation. A very high percent of the cases I deal with in my practice involve human relationships—especially close family ties. Today, family systems are constantly in flux. One in two marriages ends in divorce. There are more single-parent and step-families than first-time families.

For that reason alone, work with individuals should be more productive and have a more lasting effect—both for family groupings and for our culture as a whole—than work that focuses only on a given family situation. The exception would be when the presenting problem rests with a child, since in children's cases, it is the parents' thought that is most in need of healing.

While contextual concepts have helped fill the enormous void in moral precepts that has existed within the therapeutic field in the past, professional counsellors today generally advocate an eclectic approach that values multiple perspectives and uses a variety of methods. But my own experience lies with the spiritual perspective that acknowledges God as "man's only real relative on earth and in heaven" (Eddy 1896, 151)—as the universal Father-Mother of us all, the Source from which all good flows, and from which none of us can ever be separated.

This is the perspective I have drawn upon since early childhood. It is a perspective that has proved to be a strength, comfort, and protection to me over many decades, through many changes, and has brought me finally to a companioning grounded in spiritual oneness—an equal partnership in all that makes life worth living.

It is the fact of one's belovedness as a child of God that overcomes not only neurosis but attendant physical disorders as well. Nothing less can enable one to bear what seems unbearable: the shattering of one's fondest early hopes, the mockery of one's earnest efforts, the apparent—but always temporary—victory of injustice and strife, the unmerited scorn and cruel condemnation of those who are both ignorant and presumptive. The promise is that one who bears this cross, "will win and wear the crown" (Eddy 1906, 254).

One can seldom draw valid general conclusions from isolated particulars. Nevertheless, the lessons I've learned over many years with regard to marriage and family discords may resonate with others' needs. My own truths are these:

1) pity isn't a right basis for a lasting companionship, nor is a compulsive need to be needed. (There are, of course, many other wrong bases for marriage, such as sheer sensualism, selfishness, using marriage as an escape from unsolved problems, the expectation that another can resolve one's own sense of incompleteness, poor self-esteem or unhappiness.)

2) when a situation isn't right and doesn't rectify, one must be willing to let go of it—of what's wrong—before he can be ready for what's right, and this takes humility and courage. Pride, fear, and an incapacity to examine one's self and correct one's own errors tend to render individuals incapable of progress.

3) hypocrisy or pretense, as well as irresponsibility and inequity, undermine the integrity of any institution—certainly of marriage. Whatever isn't genuine won't survive, no matter how desperately one tries to perpetuate the sham.

4) even though a problem goes unresolved for decades, if we pray and listen for divine direction, God will guide us and will prepare us for its resolution. Moreover, divine Love will provide what is needed each step of the way.

5) we can't work out another's salvation or do his work for him; we are each responsible for our own thoughts and acts. Blaming another renders the task of self correction difficult or impossible.

6) any partnership, and all healthy relationships, must be based on mutuality of effort and commitment—one partner can't carry the whole burden for both.

7) one can companion on a journey only with another who is going in the same direction and walking at the same pace.

8) ultimately, one can always tell a tree by its fruits, or judge a situation by its consequences, and marriage can be judged by the disappointments it involves or the hopes it fulfils.

I like to think of marriage as a career which one carries on simultaneously with other careers. In a career, we have to grow, to keep qualifying. We can't go one way, and our fellow-workers another. Nor can we abandon our legitimate obligations, betray others' trust, be unfaithful to our commitments and still expect to retain our job.

It is false and outdated theology that promotes a blinding sense of duty, a false responsibility for others, and consequent guilt or burden in personal relationships. We do have a commitment, and that is to endeavor to see others as God sees them. This will either bring change and healing to a difficult situation or ultimately lift one out of it altogether.

Our necessity is to feel our individual at-one-ment with God. Out of this closeness springs comfort, guidance, support, protection, and joy.

Here is a practical view of marriage: "That it is often convenient, sometimes pleasant, and occasionally a love affair... It sometimes presents the most wretched condition of human existence. To be normal, it must be a union of the affections that tends to lift mortals higher" (Eddy 1986, 52). I also agree that "Pure humanity, friendship, home, the interchange of love, bring to earth a foretaste of heaven" (Eddy 1896, 100).

There is a divorcement that must take place before we can experience such a "foretaste of heaven." And that has to do with divorcing ourselves from unhealed errors of the past. We must each separate from our own thinking those entrenched fears, habits, attitudes, that would perpetuate a "yoking together" that is unequal, a contract that has been broken, a "co- dependence" that is unhealthy and unnatural.

Here's an example. A woman I know grew up in a family that exhibited many of the negative consequences of "destructive entitlement" and unequal and unjust power relations. Her father, the youngest of five children of German Lutheran background, lost his own mother at age four and was raised by his oldest sister. Without completing high school, he apprenticed as an electrician and then, in the early 1920's, married. Things went well until the depression hit and he lost his job. For a time their financial struggle was severe, and that's when she—the only child—was born.

The father had great difficulty verbalizing his feelings. He was possessed of a violent temper and was both emotionally and physically abusive to her and her mother. He forbade his wife to work outside the home, remaining totally in control of their finances, and for a time even prevented her attending church. The wife found solace in private prayer and in the study of Christian Science.

But the husband was unfaithful to their marriage, carrying on a relationship with another woman over a period of years, with the result that the parents separated for a time. With the help of a Christian Science practitioner, they reconciled and seemed happier.

However, when a severe business loss occurred— the result of a partner's dishonesty—her father became very disheartened and embittered. He died within a few years of a massive stroke. The marriage had lasted 32 years. The father's apparent callousness and insensitivity clearly masked the hurt child within. He was a hard worker and, with his passing, left his wife financially secure. Her second marriage to a long-time friend proved to be a great blessing to them both.

The daughter was a classic example of the "parentified child." She provided the stabilizing triangulation within the family, feeling it her responsibility to maintain home harmony. Whenever the parents weren't speaking to each other she was the go-between. Even when the parents separated, she played the peace-maker role.

When she married, she chose someone she could take care of. Because of the unhappiness in her home growing up, she nurtured such a yearning for a normal family situation, coupled with false responsibility and personal pride, that she held on for forty years to a relationship that became increasingly difficult, struggling to make everything right and pretending to herself and others that all was right, even in the face of mounting evidence to the contrary.

Most of the destructive elements in her parents' marriage eventually were replicated in her own. Numerous business re-locations and extensive business travel by her husband, especially when their children were young, as well as severe and unexplained problems with two of their children, took further toll.

Countless times over the years through earnest prayer, home harmony was restored, physical problems were healed, and financial needs were supplied. Important direction was provided and progress took place in her husband's career. But the marriage itself didn't progress. Finally she realized that what needed changing was her own concept of man, fostered in childhood, as self-absorbed, insecure, ill-tempered, sometimes violent, uncommunicative, ungrateful, even hypocritical. She worked earnestly to make this change until, on the occasion of a particularly destructive outburst, she was compelled to let go, sure of God's timing and direction. Then followed two remarkable years, bringing into her experience an unsought and deeply satisfying companionship. In time, the former husband remarried as well, and there is gratifying evidence of progress and spiritual growth for everyone involved.

Success in marriage and in life involves cleansing memory, letting go the past—its hurts, griefs, and disappointments, forsaking pretense in order to be genuine, basing forgiveness on the recognition that one's only real history or record is "on high" (Job 16:19). No child of God is simply a product of human forebears or of the circumstances of a material existence. Nor are the possibilities for one's growth forever limited or proscribed.

We can be like Paul who, "forgetting those things which are behind, and reaching forth unto those things which are before" (Phil. 3:13-14) pressed toward the prize of God's high calling. Often we're not ready to do this until we have sufficiently redeemed the past by correcting our present sense of it—seeing it from a totally new and wholly spiritual perspective. Joseph did this when he forgave the brothers who had sold him into slavery by seeing in their cruelty the working out of a divine purpose. "God sent me before you to preserve you a posterity in the earth, and to save your lives by a great deliverance...So now it was not you that sent me hither, but God (Gen. 45:7-8)...as for you, ye thought evil against me; but God meant it unto good..." (Gen. 50:20).

This doesn't mean God's will for anyone is hurtful or that suffering is ever in accord with God's purpose. Rather it indicates the power of God's will or law, through one's own fidelity and obedience to that law, to turn anything hurtful into blessing, any evil into good, any tragedy into triumph.

Many people resist change. Yet, healing is change. We can't absolutize the relative, and marriage is a relative human state. It can approach the divine by conforming to what is spiritually real. When marriage represents "two individual natures in one" (Eddy 1906, 577), when it signifies human closeness based on spiritual oneness, then it is "made in heaven"—is evidence of the divinely appointed blending and conjoining of God's ideas for mutual blessing.

In any circumstance, it's never who's right but what's right that is important. If we relate rightly to God—if we meet God's demand to hold our thought to what is spiritually true and live to the best of our ability in accord with that reality—then we'll relate to others in ways that are enhancing not degrading, that are promotive and not destructive of individual worth and universal good.

Our indestructible relationship with God is what undergirds our relationships with others. Such relationships endure and bless when they are based in Truth and Love—in what is both spiritually valid and humanly benevolent. Eventually we must come to understand the universality of God's love and each individual's worthiness to be loved. Then we won't be willing to tolerate whatever is negative or false either in ourselves or in others. Trust and one's entire sense of self-confidence must ultimately rest with this divine Love and not with a person.

To be able to act as though one is the loved of God, and not simply react; to remain undisturbed in the face of anger, violence, injustice; to keep one's own peace and poise regardless of the storms raging without; to respond with charitableness and forgiveness rather than retaliate in kind: this is the Christly way.

What then is our commitment in marriage? More than to another person or a given relationship, it is to the highest, most unselfish loving we know, and to the greatest integrity or genuineness which we are capable of expressing. Our commitment is to the increasing expression of our true selfhood and to cherishing and companioning with that spiritual or real character in another. Difficulties arise when one or both partners begin to betray that genuine selfhood. To act in a manner that denigrates or weakens another is to denigrate oneself. Such a violation robs one of both self-respect and happiness.

What can we do if we feel in need of right companionship? We can endeavor to express more of the qualities we feel are lacking in our experience—to demonstrate more of our individual completeness. We can lift our thought of ourselves and others higher and claim every individual's spiritual worth. We can labor to free ourselves from past negative imprints and to resolve old problems. We can manifest more of the Christly selfhood that is always attractive. We can turn our attention outward, finding our own in others' good. God's ideas aren't interdependent since they depend on God alone. But they are interrelated, and everyone can find kinship in mutual aims and interests, and in common efforts to bless.

Happiness really comes from within, not without, from unselfed giving to others, not from getting or from self-seeking, self-indulgence, and gratification. Whether we are married or not, whether we have families or not, whether or not we are "popular" or well-liked, whether or not our material circumstances are just as we'd prefer, we can be happy by being and doing good, and by being genuine—free of pretense, prevarication, pride, and hypocrisy.

The message God is giving each of us is the same one the father gave the eldest son in Jesus' famous parable of the Prodigal: "Son, thou art ever with me, and all that I have is thine" (Luke 15:31). We need to accept that promise, understand that God gives us all we need—that we each have all God gives (Eddy 1886, 5)—and think from the standpoint of our all-inclusiveness. "All...which thou seest, to thee will I give it, and to thy seed forever" (Gen.13:15) indicates that we must first envision or discern spiritual good and then we will have evidence of it humanly. And not only will we be blessed but all our "seed"—those who witness our truth and follow our example—will be also.

Two other points. True humility eliminates humiliation. Humility doesn't mean timidity. It doesn't mean letting others walk all over you. It means acknowledging your oneness with God—that you can of yourself do and be nothing. The truly humble know they can no more be "put down," taken advantage of, or denigrated than God can be. Humility doesn't take offense. It obliterates irritation, defuses strife, eliminates rivalry, eradicates insecurity, maintains deep inner peace.

Every emerging right idea, and that certainly includes a right relationship, needs protection from the murderous Herods of mortal thought, from the guilt-driven suspicions and malicious envy of others. Such shelter isn't deceit; it is wisdom. It means staying "hid with Christ in God" from the "strife of tongues." Any right idea carries itself forward. Everything aids the idea or is in harmony with it. We don't have to promote the idea or employ any schemes for its fulfillment. When we resort to willful human outlining or to human ways and means to advance a spiritual idea, we profoundly diminish or alter its character. Instead, we want to know that if anything is of God—is divinely right and blessed—nothing can harm or oppose it. On the other hand, whatever is not of God, is unsustainable and will inevitably fail (Acts 5:38-39). No amount of human willfulness can perpetuate it.

Spiritual Healing And Children

In recent years, there has been an aggressive attempt to remove from state statutes long-standing accommodations for the practice of spiritual healing for children. There has even been improper withholding of federal funds by the United States Department of Health and Human Services from those states that refuse to comply.

This effort has been spear-headed by a few well-publicized prosecutions of parents and others in the United

States where a child under Christian Science treatment has passed on—sometimes with and sometimes without medical attention. Rita Swan, a former Christian Scientist whose infant son died of spinal meningitis after two weeks of prayerful treatment followed by ten days in the hospital, has documented 165 cases of children who have died since 1975 "because medical care was withheld for religious reasons."

This statistic appears in an article in the April, 1995 Atlantic Monthly, but without mention of the fact that only twelve of the cases involve Christian Scientists. The article's author, Caroline Fraser, turns on her parents and her upbringing in Christian Science, with a measure of personal bitterness and bias seldom seen in major national publications.

Ms. Fraser features the story of Andrew Wantland— a 12 year-old who died suddenly in December, 1992, of a very rare and virulent form of juvenile onset diabetes. Andrew's father did call for emergency medical assistance, but both the paramedics who came to the home, and the medical center staff who treated the boy, misdiagnosed and misdrugged the child, exacerbating the diabetic shock. Andrew's mother, who had prior to this tragedy, divorced her husband and remarried, brought a multi-million dollar civil lawsuit against her former husband, Andrew's father. On March 14, 1995, an Orange County (California) Superior Court Judge ordered a complete dismissal of the suit.

Any loss—or any abuse—of a child is a tragedy. I know that the greatest anguish I have ever felt has been over my children and my failure to protect them and to provide them with the secure and spiritually grounded upbringing I tried so hard to give them. Without a doubt, what you don't know has power to harm you. As others have seen:

"Ignorance of the error to be eradicated oftentimes subjects you to its abuse" (Eddy 1906, 446). Such ignorance becomes a ready channel through which deliberate hatred, envy, or malice can operate.

The fact remains that such child deaths are rare among Christian Scientists, and usually involve conditions considered medically treatable but incurable. A case in point is the much publicized prosecution in Boston of the Twitchells for "negligence" in the death of their two-year old son of a bowel obstruction. Almost no mention was made in the newspapers of the fact that this condition was due to a rare birth defect (found by autopsy), or that children die of this same problem under medical treatment. Moreover, the presiding judge allowed no testimony in court of verifiable healings by means of Christian Science treatment.

Carolyn Fraser comments in regard to the Twitchell case: "...at the time the prosecutors got exactly what they intended. Even though the conviction was later overturned on appeal, it fixed in the public mind an image of irresponsible Christian Science practices." This comment indicates that not facts, but impressions or "images" are paramount.

Certainly it appears that the aim of such prosecutions is not just welfare of children, since the over-all record of Christian Science healing compares very favorably with the record of recovery by medical means. We can only presume that by challenging freedom of religious practice and the right to choose a proven alternative method, certain interests hope either to establish a medical monopoly or to destroy the foundation and future growth of the movement toward spiritual means in healing.

A larger evil than personal bitterness or malice is involved. That is the effort in our secular society to destroy innocence, to contaminate and adulterate purity, even to destroy the very spiritual and moral foundations upon which this nation was built. This evil would use children either as vehicles for evil doing or make them targets for hatred and abusiveness.

My peace has come from earnest efforts to overcome my own ignorance, to be more disciplined, more genuine and faithful in my own life and practice, as well as from letting God be Mother. By this I mean the recognition that no one can be god to another. Although parents can't be excused for neglect or lack of proper care of those in their charge, ultimately each individual belongs to, is obligated to and governed by the sole Parent we call God. The security, guidance and protection we each need comes from bonding, not with a person, but with our common divine Source. And what God does is forever: "nothing can be put to it, nor any thing taken from it" (Eccl.3:14). No circumstance, however brutal, can set aside God's will for any of us, stay God's hand or purpose, or nullify God's blessing. Sooner or later, we must each look Godward and at least glimpse and begin to recover our innate spiritual wholeness.

It takes wisdom and alertness, as well as humility and inoffensiveness, to render deliberate hatred ineffective and to forestall or nullify its consequences. The fact is, the movement toward spiritual healing can't be stopped. That movement has spread far beyond the numerically few Christian Scientists and is thriving in churches everywhere.

There is widespread recognition today that health or wholeness and holiness are inseverably linked. Moreover many thoughtful individuals are questioning the medical record. Despite highly vaunted medical "miracles," the fact remains that more than a third of the patients on general medical services are suffering from diseases related to medical intervention. Further, more than 100,000 deaths each year in the United States are a direct result of hospital acquired infections from the use of antibiotics (Inlander, Levin, and Weiner 1988, 124-143). Such statistics appear in many publications today, including the New England Journal of Medicine.

An interview with Dr. Jer Master, a pediatrician from Bombay, India, was published in the April, 1980 Christian Science Journal. Over a ten year period, Dr. Master gradually left medical practice and is now a Christian Science practitioner. Asked about what she saw as differences between Christian Science practice and medical practice she replied: "First, medical theories change from year to year. Books written 10 years ago are almost outdated now. There's not a fixed law on which such theories are based, whereas Christian Science is based on fixed Principle...

"Secondly, medicines and drugs frequently have dangerous side effects, whereas the effects of Christian Science treatment are wholly beneficial. Finally, each case in Christian Science is highly specific. Medically, you might treat ten children who had the same illness with the same medication. But there may be ten different fears...that need to be reversed (or circumstances that need to be dealt with.) You can handle them specifically in Christian Science" (Master 1980, 175-178).

Dr. Master has since lectured extensively throughout the world on her experiences. In a 1989 lecture, as reported in the Christian Science Sentinel, she mentions an experience of a little girl who was at home alone with her grandmother.

The grandmother suddenly fell ill, so ill she couldn't even move or go to the door and call anyone. She asked her little granddaughter to pray for her. The little girl told her grandmother: "God loves you, He didn't make you sick." The child's simple faith and fundamental grasp of God's goodness helped the grandmother recover quickly. Dr. Master's point was that Christian Science isn't a difficult philosophy. Anyone with a child's purity and simplicity can understand and practice it.

Dr. Master concludes her lecture: "Christian Science is open to everyone and anyone. It is a wonderful message of hope, and it doesn't matter if you think of yourself as worthy or unworthy; whether you are an addict or convict; or belonging to any religion, (or) uneducated... It is available to everyone... Thought is opening up...The power of prayer is being accepted... God...works in ways which sometimes are so silent we are not aware of it. But the changes are there, happening all over the world" (Master 18 June, 1990, 24-27).

Certainly, children in this country are at risk today from the glaring absence of spiritual or moral values in their up-bringing, and from parents' failure to live what they preach. Children suffer from a secular culture obsessively focused on the physical and material and lacking fundamental meaning or ethical standards. Children also suffer from the notion that drugs—whether medical or social—can supply all the answers, or can spare them the consequences of self-destructive behaviors. Children suffer most from confusion about identity and its purpose, and from the pervasive and abusive influence of media indoctrination. And sometimes they suffer because no alternative to medical or psychological pronouncements of incurability is either known or available.

The remarkable healing of a three-year-old who had been hit by a car was published in The Christian Science Sentinel. A Christian Science practitioner was called by the child's grandfather, who had custody of his little grandson and was raising him. When the practitioner arrived at the hospital, the picture was not good. Neither was the doctor's diagnosis which included internal injuries, brain damage, and multiple bruises. The doctor doubted that the boy would ever regain consciousness, much less survive. No medication was given to the child. After two weeks, the boy was released from the hospital with the verdict that nothing more could be done for him.

Loving provision was found for the child in the home of a Christian Science family, and prayer was continued. The child by this time had regained full consciousness but was not able to walk or talk. One day when the practitioner came to visit, she knelt down to the level of his little chair several feet away and held out her arms to him. He stood up and walked to her. Putting his arms around her neck, he said, 'I love you.' That was the end of the child's injuries. The next time the practitioner visited, the boy was out playing ball with other children, completely normal and healthy (Poyser 1995, 3-7).

Parents who rely on Christian Science for healing do so because they have reason to have confidence in God's promises. They have glimpsed something of each child's eternal inseparability from Life and Love, and have learned to look beyond the evidence of the physical senses. They have had abundant proof that "with God all things are

possible," (Matt.19:26) and that, whatever the spiritual fact
is, the disturbed human sense of things must conform to it.

Nothing at all can humanly control or put a stop to
such spiritual power and to the faith it engenders, as has
recently been shown in many of the former Communist
countries. The carnal mind that is "enmity against God" will
ultimately fail in every attempt to rob humanity of its true
spirituality and destiny. As Paul puts it: "The law of the Spirit
of life in Christ Jesus hath made me free from the law of sin
and death... Because the creature itself also shall be delivered
from the bondage of corruption into the glorious liberty of
the children of God" (Rom.8:2,21).

We all must sometime recognize that God is the only
Mother-Father and that we are all God's children, safe in
Love's keeping. No matter how tragic, unjust, brutal,
traumatizing the events of the human experience—and
admittedly when these events occur in a child's experience
without anyone to help make sense of what happens the effect
is more devastating and difficult to overcome—the fact
remains that God never abandons us, never betrays us, never
neglects or abuses us.

A divine influence is with us in the midst of any
fiery trial, as it was with the three Hebrew boys in the
Babylonian furnace. With divine help we can emerge
unscathed, unaffected, without even the smell of smoke,
having no need to continually rehearse the trauma, to
replicate or repeat it, to allow it to determine our outlook, to
warp our perspectives, to make us insecure, imbued with
self-pity or self-doubt.

Too many therapies entrench in individuals the sense
of being victims and of having to aggressively assert their
own rights or entitlements in order to take control of their

own lives. In fact, what those who have suffered most need is to recognize and experience God's control and ability to lift them beyond the reach of human wrath and to empower them to bless others.

As so many of the experiences shared in this chapter indicate, the choice to be made ultimately is for the best, the highest, the most spiritual and inspired sense of being. That choice alone enables us to emerge from challenges not scarred, angry, defensive, bitter, wounded, depressed, but strengthened, refined, purified. Out of that choice comes a clearer sense of our own imperishable worth and continuing purpose, as well as our ability to love and respond to love freely, to live in and make the most of each present opportunity.

Lines from a familiar hymn (Christian Science Hymnal, No. 12) state well the challenge and the promise:

"Arise ye people, take your stand,
Cast out your idols from the land,
Above all doctrine, form or creed
Is found the Truth that meets your need...

Go forward then, and as ye preach
So let your works confirm your speech...
In love and healing ministry
Show forth the Truth that makes men free.

O Father-Mother God, whose plan
Hath given dominion unto man,
In Thine own image we may see
Man pure and upright, whole and free.
And ever through our work shall shine
That light whose glory, Lord, is Thine."

Violet Hay

Chapter Five

LARGER PERSPECTIVES

"the leaves of the tree were for the healing of the nations"
(Rev. 22:2)

Extraordinary challenges always call forth individuals, some of them quite ordinary, who are able to rise to meet these challenges with extraordinary courage, compassion, and fortitude.

Often their examples, and their determination to surmount a crisis and not be victimized by it, give strength to others, occasionally even to entire communities or nations. Even one individual's transcendence over injustice or surmounting of tragedy can inspire healing or transformation for all those within the context of that experience, and sometimes far beyond it. The experience of Anne Frank as recorded in her unforgettable Diary is a case in point. Another is that of Corrie Ten Boom in The Hiding Place.

What seems requisite to such overcoming is a self-forgetful love springing out of trust in a standard of right regulating human destiny, even the conviction of a divine purpose transcending or overriding the worst human cruelty or misfortune.

The wonderful thing is that there are countless individuals, mostly unknown and unsung, whose spiritually based choices and actions have brought hope, inspiration, and healing to others. Every one has the opportunity to make such choices. Yes, our healing is up to us, as Wayne Muller states (Muller 1992, 182). But it is also our gift to others, as well as the way we honor the One who has made us and bear witness to the spirit of Truth and Love working within us.

War-Related Trauma

Like Jim Stockdale, the senior United States Naval officer held prisoner in Viet Nam during the Vietnamese conflict, John Wyndham was imprisoned by the Japanese on Java during World War II. His Australian Passport with military photo, together with a personal diary in which he had written a prediction of Japanese defeat, led to his being charged as a spy and threatened with execution.

Also like Jim Stockdale, John experienced an initial period of solitary confinement coupled with threats, deprivation, and interrogation. At one point, food and water were withheld from him for an entire week. He too was a man of strong faith and spiritual convictions. Even before his captivity John had become convinced that one's thinking determines his experience. Under the duress of imprisonment, he saw that the greatest challenge he faced was simply to control his thinking—that is, to refuse to entertain fearful, resentful, hateful suggestions

His certainty that, despite the circumstances, God alone was in control, and his determination to act in a Christian manner even if it placed his own life in jeopardy, gradually earned him the respect and trust of the guards. John spent more than three years in captivity—compared to Jim Stockdale's seven and a half years. But both men learned the absolute necessity of staying alert to audible and inaudible mental influences.

As Christmas approached one year, at the request of the prison doctor, John approached the commandant with the request that money collected from the prisoners be used to purchase fruit from near-by villagers especially for the benefit of those who were ill. He tried as best he could despite language barriers to convey something of the Christ message of peace and good-will. The result was that the commandant obtained baskets of fruit that he paid for himself.

On a number of occasions, prisoners were sent by ships to camps inside Japan—a hazardous ordeal, but each time John's name appeared on the lists of those to be sent, it was removed by the translator who had become interested in translating the book John always used along with his Bible: Science and Health with Key to the Scriptures.

As the years of hardship and deprivation wore on, many of the prisoners, a majority of whom were Australians, succumbed to despondence, illness, and a lack of will to survive. On April 25, celebrated as ANZAC Day in Australia and New Zealand, John secured the commandant's permission for the bugler to sound the "Last Post" precisely at 11 AM, at which time all the prisoners would lay down their tools and stand at attention for one minute. The remarkable thing was that all the guards also stood at attention. From that moment on the mental depression was broken.

During those prison years, John resolved to commit his life to God. Following the war's end and his release, through a series of remarkable circumstances, John was led into training as a photographer, and eventually became general manager of a photographic business in Australia. But then, he felt impelled to leave Australia, spend two weeks taking religious instruction in San Francisco, stop in New York for an expected job offer with the United Nations, and go on to Holland to visit family. The costs of this journey necessitated his selling even his camera equipment.

But the job offer was not forthcoming, and John encountered severe family difficulties in Holland. An accident ensued which left John with an incapacitated left arm and severe pain in his side. He struggled with doubt, with self-will, self-pity and resentment, but through prayer overcame these negative mental states and the physical disability as well. After a short stay in Canada, he eventually took his family to England and there began receiving so many calls for help in Christian Science that he was soon established in the full time healing practice. Still there were challenges with regard to supply and lessons to learn in not outlining how his needs were to be met. He writes: "I learned that supply truly comes from God, that it may come through people but not from people" (Wyndham 1994, 111).

He then received an offer of a two-year contract as Assistant Director of Public Information for UNICEF in New York, which he accepted. His travels for UNICEF and his contacts with peoples all over the world, as well as his efforts to resolve daily conflicts of interest among them, led him to the conclusion that the UN ideal: peace and prosperity for all peoples through the unifying of the nations, could not be achieved solely by human means. Such an ideal had to rest on a spiritual basis and be spiritually accomplished.

Following his years with UNICEF, John made his home in Los Angeles and spent the next 21 years as a practitioner and teacher of Christian Science. In l968 he was appointed to lecture, and spoke to audiences all over the United States and in many countries abroad. The promise he made to himself while in prison camp—to live his life in God's service—was fulfilled.

A self-styled "ordinary person," Margaret Powell received an urgent call at home in Pennsylvania on April 18, 1983. It was from the State Department, confirming that her brother-in-law, who was with the Agency for International Development in Beirut, had been killed earlier that day when a bomb exploded at the American Embassy. Her sister, Mary Lee, a teacher at the American University in Beirut, was in surgery at a hospital in Beirut and listed in critical condition.

After contacting her sister's three children attending school in the United States and answering many callers, Margaret was asked by the American Ambassador to go immediately to Beirut to be with her sister. She went—the only civilian with the official American delegation.

Arriving in Beirut after 20 hours of travel and prayer, Margaret went straight to the hospital. The doctors' fear that Mary Lou would lose an eye had turned into rejoicing that she would not. Within a few days, Margaret had to go to the temporary headquarters of the embassy for papers to be signed. Passing by the spectacle of the bombed out embassy building and learning more of the details of the tragedy—including the fact that a Lebanese driver had carried her sister down four flights of stairs to get her out of the building—seemed overwhelming for Margaret. But then she walked over to a group of young Marines guarding the building and was tenderly embraced by each of them. And she thought: "Here is Love, right here in the presence of this awful symbol...Strong and alive and beautiful and ready to be expressed" (Christian Science Sentinel, 20 January, 1986).

That night, however, a rumor that the hospital was the next target for bombing rapidly turned apprehension into terror. Margaret turned to the Bible, especially the 91st Psalm. Gradually, her thought changed from fear to love—

for her sister, for all those in the hospital, for the entire city and country. She prayed for all the brave people in Lebanon trying in their own way to seek peace.

She writes: "I felt more and more sure of God's love, that it can know no bounds. After many hours I saw that this love had to include those I wouldn't have thought of including—the very ones who might be contemplating further destruction. It took the whole long night to see that there is no exception to the spirituality of man... I knew that they were God's loved children... I felt peace. And it was dawn...I felt a quiet, quiet, gentle joy."

The sisters returned to the States. Mary Lou recovered fully, even to normal vision in the affected eye, and then returned overseas to serve as a government Foreign Service Officer. Margaret has since spoken to a number of church groups on the power of prayer and forgiveness, and has published an account of her experience entitled "Forgiveness in Beirut."

Social Injustice

In l957, fifteen year old Melba Beals and eight other black teenagers, in response to a Federal Court order, integrated Central High School in Little Rock, Arkansas. They ran a gauntlet flanked by a rampaging mob and the heavily armed Arkansas National Guard. Opposition to this integration was so intense that President Eisenhower was forced to call in soldiers from the elite l0lst Airborne Division to restore order.

Warriors Don't Cry is drawn from Melba Beals' personal diaries. But the pain of her memories remained so vivid it took over 35 years before she could complete her manuscript and tell her story without bitterness. That year, 1957, was filled with personal threats, brigades of attacking mothers, rogue police, fireball and acid-throwing attacks, the threat that her mother would lose her job as an English teacher unless Melba was withdrawn from school, and even a price on Melba's head.

That Melba survived with indestructible faith, courage, strength and hope is a tribute to her mother and grandmother, and to those in her church who stood with her. Not all in her black community supported the integration effort; many feared reprisals. The ultimate success of the effort was due to the fearlessness and persistence of Thurgood Marshall of the NAACP, and to the children who endured a barrage of hatred and abuse that would overwhelm most adults.

When Melba cried because of loneliness and cruelty, her grandmother insisted: "You can never in this lifetime count on another human being to keep you from being lonely. Nobody can provide your spiritual food..." (Beals 1994, 209). When she had to return home after being pelted with raw eggs one morning, her grandmother counselled: "Embarrassment is not a life-threatening problem... Dignity is a state of mind, just like freedom. These are both precious gifts from God that no one can take away unless you allow them to" (Ibid. 242).

Her grandmother helped Melba see that when she refused to react to insults or injuries—when she refused to be a victim—then she would be defeating the attackers' purpose. Finally Melba reached a point where she no longer allowed hecklers' behavior to frighten her into reacting a certain way. She began to have a powerful feeling of being in control. This inner strength carried her to the close of the school year. Yet, all the struggle seemed in vain when Governor Faubus closed all of Little Rock's High Schools the following autumn, preventing Melba and the others from returning for a senior year.

Meanwhile, black people lost jobs, homes, businesses, as pressure was exerted to convince the families to voluntarily withdraw their children. In fact, Melba, like others, was sent out of state, completing her education in Santa Rosa, California with a white family of dedicated Quakers. Melba speaks of that family as the "loving, nurturing bridge over which I walked to adulthood. More than their guidance, it was their unconditional love that taught me the true meaning of equality" (Beals 1994, 307-308). Not until the following year were two black students readmitted to Central High School and finally graduated.

Today, after degrees from San Francisco State and Columbia University and work as a reporter for NBC, Melba Beals is a communications consultant in San Francisco. The task that remains, she feels, is for each of us to see ourselves reflected in every other human being and to respect and honor our differences.

The towering figure in South Africa's struggle toward wholeness and democracy has been Nelson Mandela. At the conclusion of his trial for treason in 1963, Mandela declared to the court: "During my lifetime, I have dedicated myself to this struggle of the African people. I have fought against white domination, and I have fought against black domination. I have cherished the ideal of a democratic and free society in which all persons live together in harmony and with equal opportunities. It is an ideal which I hope to live for and to achieve. But if needs be it is an ideal for which I am prepared to die" (Benson 1994, 159).

Conviction for treason carried the death penalty, but the sentence pronounced on Mandela and four others (the Rivonia five) was life imprisonment, influenced no doubt by growing pressure from abroad. Actually his incarceration by the South African government—some of it at hard labor—totalled 27 years. Despite this, Mandela emerged from prison in 1990 with dignity and magnanimity, and in April, 1994, at South Africa's first all-racial democratic elections, and at the age of 76, he was elected President.

Despite deliberately fomented violence during the preceding months, election day, April 27, 1994, was described by official election officers as "a spiritual experience, a freeing experience." In a nation where 78 per cent of the population profess to be Christians, many had been praying for a harmonious outcome. One Russian observer remarked, "What has happened here has been a miracle." A white professor at Stellenbosch University said he felt voting was like an act of atonement. Agnes Hofmeyr, a South African author living in Johannesburg, remarked, "Dignity is restored to the masses. The humiliations and hurts of the past forgiven are the solid foundation on which the future will be built" (Christian Science Sentinel, 29 August, 1994, 7-10).

Along with Mandela's overwhelming victory as President came the transformation of the South African Parliament—a change as astounding as the earlier collapse of Communism in Eastern Europe and within the Soviet Union. Enormous tasks remain as these countries seek to rebuild on a just and spiritual basis. The Biblical promise is that "He which hath begun a good work in you will complete it unto the day of Christ" (Phil.1:6).

Mandela has always stood, even against some of his black compatriots, for the inclusion of people of all races and persuasions in the struggle for political equality. He is a committed Christian, a Methodist church member.

What has happened in South Africa since 1994 bears out Mandela's remarks to a huge crowd assembled at the city hall in Cape Town on the occasion of his release from prison in February, 1990: "Your tireless and heroic sacrifices have made it possible for me to be here... I place the remaining years of my life in your hands." One foreign correspondent covering the occasion wrote: "Mandela's lack of bitterness, inner calm and certainty were so unexpected, it was quite overpowering" (Benson 1994, 254-255).

Subsequent events indicate that, in even the most difficult and apparently intransigent situations, right ultimately must prevail. Whatever is moral or nearest right humanly is spiritually impelled and divinely protected. Even in the face of the most determined resistance, progress in the direction of justice must take place. Jeremiah declares: "I know the thoughts that I think toward you, saith the Lord, thoughts of peace, and not of evil, to give you an expected end" (29:11)—the expected fulfilment of spiritually-based hopes, coupled with an end to humanly instigated and perpetuated wrongs.

Criminal Violence

Most people transfixed by the televised repetition of the videotaped beating of Rodney King are aware that the not guilty verdict in the Simi Valley trial of four Los Angeles Police officers involved in that beating led to

tremendous outbreaks of violence in the black neighborhoods
of Los Angeles.

Another picture, hard to eradicate from memory, was
that of the near fatal attack on truck driver Reginald Denny,
who was pulled from his truck at the intersection of Florence
and Normandie Avenues on April 29, 1992 soon after the
verdict became known. At the subsequent trial of the
attackers, Henry Keith Watson and Damian Williams, Denny
described the scene as "total madness;" his skull was broken
into over 100 fragments in the attack.

Although many people felt the jury's acquittal of
Damian Williams on attempted murder charges too lenient,
Denny himself—who had been rescued that day by four
Angelenos of extraordinary courage—was most forgiving.
He declined to appeal, saying that he was in total agreement
with the verdicts, and adding: "Let's get on with life." Most
touching was his courtroom embrace of Williams' mother—
a gesture which totally diffused any further vindictiveness
(Los Angeles Times, 19 and 21 October, 1993).

Such forgiveness was strikingly present in a bombing
by terrorists in Northern Ireland in 1987. In the border town
of Enniskillen, where innocent people had gathered to pay
respects at a war memorial, a bomb went off, killing eleven
people, one of whom was a twenty-year-old student nurse,
Marie Wilson. That same night, Marie's father, who was with
her when the bomb exploded, was interviewed. His response
touched millions. "I bear no grudge," he said. "God is good,
and we shall meet again."

In a book he wrote following the incident, Gordon
Wilson declares that he and his wife Joan were aware that
night of a level of prayer that was palpable. His further
comment to the reporter that he would pray every night for

those who had planted the bomb that God will forgive them, made him a voice for peace and hope in Northern Ireland.

In 1993 Mr. Wilson was invited by the Prime Minister of Ireland to become an independent member of the Senate in Dublin. He has since met face-to-face with terrorists and asked them to consider non-violent ways of achieving their objectives. His example has helped many let go of the past and move toward a negotiated settlement.

When telling Marie's story, he refers to it as a "love story," since her last words were not of selfishness, or anger, or of blame but of her love for him. The lesson of Enniskillen, he insists, is that hatred was not allowed to triumph. He often calls attention to Jesus' two great commands (Matt.22:37-39), and points out that our "neighbor" includes Protestant, Catholic, and even terrorist (Christian Science Sentinel, 17 October, 1994, 19-22).

Without a doubt, Mr. Wilson's faith and forgiveness have helped to set in motion a healing process that is still going on and that must ultimately benefit all.

Physical And Financial Disability

The story of "Brother Andrew" told in the book God's Smuggler copyrighted in 1967 is the story of a Dutch boy who grew up in modest circumstances in the small town of Witte and survived the deprivations of the German occupation, only to enlist in the Dutch Army at the age of 17 in Holland's unsuccessful struggle to retain the Dutch East India (Indonesian) colonies.

The fighting in Indonesia left him crippled—barely able to walk without great pain, a tragedy to one whose greatest joy and skill was running. But it also turned him to his mother's Bible. After his return home at the age of 21, Andrew struggled with fierce pride, gnawing guilt, growing resentment of his handicap and uncertainty about his future, until late one night, up in his bed under the eaves, he let go. He let go his ego—his own personal sense of will or capacity, and quietly turned himself over to God. Thus began his freedom, and his remarkable journey.

A few weeks later in Amsterdam at a meeting conducted by a well-known Dutch evangelist, he made a commitment to serve God as a missionary. This commitment would ultimately cost him the support of the girl he had hoped to marry. His first challenge—and conversion—came in the Dutch chocolate factory where he worked. A profane, scornful, and belligerent woman worker experienced a total change of attitude and outlook. Soon, Andrew advanced into a two year management training program, but his heart was already committed to the training requisite for his missionary goal.

The way seemed difficult and uncertain. One Sunday in September, 1952, he went out into the polders (fields reclaimed from the sea) to pray and remained there into the evening. His prayer finally moved from Yes, but... "I'm not educated" or "I'm lame" or "I haven't the means" to an unqualified "Yes. I'll go, Lord...Whenever, wherever, however You want me, I'll go... As I stand up from this place...will You consider that this is a step toward complete obedience?..." (Andrew 1967, 55).

As Andrew stood up to return for a Sunday evening church service, he felt a sharp wrench in his leg. Testing, he found he could put weight on the injured leg and walk normally, without pain. He walked joyously to the meeting six kilometers away, and then home to his family. The next day at work old stitches came out through the skin of his ankle, and the incision, which had never healed properly, at last closed. He was completely healed. The following week he applied for admission to the Worldwide Evangelization Crusade Missionary Training College in Glasgow, and was accepted to start the following May.

Despite a final break with his girlfriend and last minute word from the college that the expected vacancy had not materialized, as well as concern over his ability to train in English, Andrew left in obedience to the inner, small voice that said "Go." Then followed a remarkable several months of learning, not just understandable English, but lifelong lessons in God's ability to meet human needs through faith and practical loving kindness.

A place opened up for him at the College, and throughout his two years of training in Glasgow, Andrew never lacked for tuition funds, although he had entered the college with just enough for the first term. On one occasion, he and four others were sent out on a month long tour with a one pound banknote between them. They returned, having their needs fully supplied by unsolicited contributions and having given away a tithe of whatever they received. All their lessons turned on trusting God's Word and on absolute obedience to God's direction.

Just before graduation, Andrew happened to see in a magazine an ad for a Communist youth festival to be held in Warsaw in July. He wrote of his desire to attend as a Christian missionary and was invited to come. He did attend carrying a suitcase loaded with Biblical tracts. At the conclusion of the festival, during which he was able to visit church services of several denominations, he felt a clear leading from God to "strengthen the things which remain

that are ready to die" (Rev.3:2). His calling, he felt, was to
the struggling remnant of believers behind the Iron Curtain.
And he felt sure God would provide the way.

At the invitation of Dutch Communists, his next visit
was to Czechoslovakia. There he learned first hand that the
need was for Bibles. None could be purchased on the excuse
that a "new translation" was being prepared. The government
controlled the churches by licensing all ministers and
reviewing their sermons, as well as selecting all students at
theological schools.

In the fall of 1956 came the Hungarian Revolt,
followed by a flood of refugees into camps in West Germany
and Austria. Andrew visited these camps, bringing aid and
hope to people destitute of the most basic necessities. Soon
thereafter, he was led to apply once more for a Yugoslavian
visa that had been previously refused. This time, applying
from Berlin, it was granted.

So it was that in 1957, Andrew passed across the
Yugoslav border in a small Volkswagen bulging with hidden
Bibles and tracts. Then followed a most remarkable 50 days,
during which time Andrew spoke to Christian groups more
than 80 times, distributing what he had brought. The car and
needed funds were supplied by Christian friends in Holland.
Near the end of his visit while in Belgrade in May, Andrew's
resolve grew: to bring Bibles to people deprived of them in
every place where God opened the door.

Since that time to the present day, this purpose has
been fulfilled—first in the "outer ring" of Communist
countries in Europe, then in the "inner ring," where there
was least freedom to worship. Andrew's mission has reached
from Russia itself, to Cuba and Albania, and currently to
wherever persecution of Christian believers is greatest: to

China and various Islamic countries. Time and again on these journeys, remarkable and unplanned helpful coincidences, guidance, protection, and provision have been experienced.

Andrew's repeated prayer for companionship was answered in his marriage in 1958 to Corrie van Dam, a fellow Christian he had met while working at the Ringer chocolate factory in Alkmaar. Soon after their marriage, while he was on a dangerous mission into Bulgaria via Greece, Andrew experienced a fear and depression such as he had never before known, compounded by crippling physical pain in his back. Coming upon the ancient Greek town of Philippi, he paused to think of Paul and Silas imprisoned in this very place, and of God's deliverance of them. He writes: "The bonds of depression that had wrapped themselves around me snapped as had the chains on Paul's wrists. The spirit of heaviness lifted, and as it did I realized with a start that I was standing erect... Joy welled up in me, physical joy as well as mental" (Andrew 1967, 140). He had experienced his own deliverance, as well as renewed strength and courage.

Of special interest in his unfolding story is Andrew's maturing concept of God's bountiful care. Time and again, his needs, and those of his growing family, were met. But he began to realize that he was depending on one "emergency dispensation" after another to get him out of a tight financial spot "instead of leaning back in the arms of a Father Who had more than enough and to spare."

Years of skimping and frugality, he saw, had developed into an "attitude of lack"—a "dark, brooding, pinched attitude that hardly went with the Christ of the open heart that we were preaching to others." He and Corrie began to take joy in God's provision, and learned a lesson in abundance—not just in terms of a home for their family and needed physical things, but in terms of others who could help carry on the work.

Ultimately, their small "organism" of twelve closely knit workers began training other missionaries, and the work has changed and expanded in response to changing times and needs. But the over-riding impression one gains from his book, as well as from the bimonthly magazine," Open Doors," published by his worldwide organization, is that when one is willing and obedient, God does the rest. As Andrew puts it: "...God is never defeated...the ultimate outcome can never be in doubt. Every day we see fresh proof that indeed all things—even evil ones—work together for those who are called by His name" (Andrew 1967, 223).

Role Of The Media

A sizeable majority of Americans agree with former Senator Bob Dole's criticisms of the excessive sex and violence portrayed by the American entertainment industry (as reported in a Los Angeles Times poll, June 14, 1995). President Clinton and others raised their voices following the Oklahoma City bombing to question whether the right to free speech doesn't carry with it certain responsibilities. A Congressional Hearing chaired by Senator Arlan Specter of Pennsylvania investigated the militia movement and its rhetoric. Possibly such a movement would not have arisen except for the failure of government—particularly the legal system—to deal effectively with crime, as well as other governmental intrusions or mistakes perceived as excessive. The tragedy at the Branch Davidian compound in Waco, Texas has become a symbol of the general breakdown of public trust in law-enforcement.

While considering the effect for good one individual's life and example may have on others, should we not also conversely consider the toxic effect accruing from words that inflame, from pictures that startle and dismay, from the constant stream of mindless violence and meaningless sex poured into public thought by film, broadcast, and recording industries? Even children's video games today have to be screened for content, and computer communications monitored.

What's needed is a growing recognition of the fact that thought governs experience. Belief, attitude, value, feeling, understanding cannot be severed from action or consequence. Job put it succinctly when he declared: "The thing which I greatly feared is come upon me" (Job 3:25). This fact underlies the constant tension between media producers who sell advertising based on the numbers of viewers or listeners they hope to attract by means of the lurid and sensational, and the public good on the other. It also raises questions relative to the constant prediction and portrayal of disease and disaster under the guise of needed public information, when it is actually pharmaceutical producers and medical facilities and practitioners or particular investors that reap the ensuing financial benefits.

The saving factor is informed choice. As cable channels proliferate, as record and video production capacity disseminates more widely, as desk-top publishing expands, and as computer-based communication capacities explode, a viable alternative will exist in value-based and responsible Christian broadcasting, and in a greater range of choices by concerned consumers. Another remedy may grow out of a greater mutual appreciation and dialogue between religion and the media.

An example of such appreciation was given in an interview with Peggy Wehmeyer who appears, though infrequently, on ABC's World News Tonight. She spoke frankly of general public concern over the tremendous decay in morals and values in this country, coupled with a resurgence of interest in spirituality. Her own goal in reporting, she said, is to be "in this world but not of it." She concluded: "You need to have discipline in your life as you make your own spiritual journey. At the same time, you must walk in the world with tremendous love and humility, so that you can represent God in a way that's worthy of your calling as His child" (Christian Science Sentinel, February 20, 1995, 11-13).

Words and ideas (whether visual, audible, or textual) are potent weapons that need to be used honestly, responsibly, and creatively. As media techniques become more sophisticated and media influence ever more persuasive, the viewing and listening public needs to learn mental defense. We need to be careful and alert evaluators of the suggestions or impressions that present themselves to us often very beguilingly, sometimes very aggressively. Much "disinformation" needs to be countered with fact.

Mental Defense

Mental suggestions of all sorts continually knock at the door of consciousness. Therefore, we must learn how to distinguish between our own true God-derived thoughts, and the suggestions that emanate from world belief and that seek, either ignorantly or deliberately, to influence us negatively. Such mental defense requires vigilance and a clear standard of values, as well as a grasp of the nature of hypnotic suggestion and the methods of mental manipulation.

Jesus' teaching was to tell "false prophets" by their fruits (Matt.7:15-18). There has always been preaching without practice as well as self-serving pretense. Anciently as today and in diverse cultures, there have been people trained in secret methods of indoctrination, of brainwashing or mental control. Nothing but diligent attunement to the divine Mind—nothing but keeping ourselves in the love of God—will furnish humanity adequate and consistent defense against such manipulation.

Does that mean God knows or allows evil? No, it doesn't. If the infinite Mind did know (or purpose and allow) evil, then we could never hope to overcome evil or be free of it, since what Deity knows is forever. If we thought that God's purpose included suffering or tragedy, disease or disaster, or even various forms of mental control, then what would be the point of resisting such ills? Light doesn't—and can't— know darkness. Yet, light by its very nature dispels darkness.

Disease, famine, senseless violence or tragedy, ignorant or deliberate malice and abusiveness, human will and mental or physical tyranny are not of God, nor do they occur with divine sanction. No matter how evil appears to succeed, it is ultimately unreal—powerless and self-destructive. Only what is allied to the divine nature and purpose endures. Christliness or godliness is not only triumphant over human wrong; it is our genuine selfhood.

What we are is primary. That will not only communicate more loudly and powerfully than what we say, but it also constitutes our protection. If our lives represent God or Truth, if they hint what is spiritually real in a way that is worthy, this will convey itself and will inspire and bless in the way of God's appointing. It will also constitute our immunity to any moral or mental contagion and our defense against the consequences of the belief in a power apart from God. It will nullify the world's hatred of or resistance to Truth. Jesus didn't do away with that hatred, but he proved it powerless.

Our capacity to detect and eliminate whatever is evil or erroneous rests on our ability to be conscious of truth and good—to be conscious of what is spiritually real. An evil suggestion can't enter a thought imbued with good. To "handle" an error is to detect it as error; then to rebuke and replace it with truth. When error is ruled out of thought, it can't appear or continue to be manifest as experience. That's why evil's most vicious lie is that we can't think rightly— that we can't control our thinking.

But we always can. Adele Blok's experience illustrates this point. As a young woman, Adele had been searching for truth—especially for the reality of her own identity. She was early absorbed in works on metaphysics, philosophy, and religion. Her parents combined European, Indonesian, and Chinese ancestry, although both her mother and father were of Dutch nationality.

She and her sister were educated in Europe—in Holland, Vienna and Paris—just before the outbreak of World War II. On returning to their home in Bandung, Adele was torn by sorrow and rebellion, questioning the nature of God and the evidence of evil taking place in the world. Though Indonesia came under Japanese rule as a result of the War, there was a concurrent movement toward independence from Dutch colonialism, and she became involved in political action, describing herself as "a deeply dissatisfied human being" (Babbitt 1975, 8).

Most Dutch Indonesians were suspect by the Japanese, and Adele and her sister were arrested and imprisoned for several months. During this time, as a result of much self-searching, Adele felt a greater inner peace, and a growing determination to devote her life to helping others find freedom from oppression. Soon after her release, she moved to Jakarta and encountered a mystic who asked to give her lessons. What ensued taught her much about the nature of mental domination and our need and ability to resist it.

Arrested again and detained in sub-human conditions, she came close to a mental breaking-point. The temptation was to escape through insanity. She felt justified in so doing, and even a sort of satisfaction because others would have to recognize how much she had suffered. But with sudden determination, she turned on this suggestion and resisted it, refusing ever to admit that evil is stronger than good. This broke the mesmerism.

She was released, and soon thereafter was given a copy of the Christian Science textbook. Through it she glimpsed for the first time that to follow Christ is to know the Truth and bear witness to it as Jesus did. She saw that not mere faith in Jesus but an understanding of God and of the true spiritual nature of man brings healing—frees from injustices of every kind. She had found her true identity and her mission in life.

Soon after the War's end, she and a few others began holding Christian Science church services. Thereafter she became a public practitioner and teacher of Christian Science, dedicated to the spiritual development of her patients and students. Many of these students played a role in the subsequent internal struggle in Indonesia, not just for independence from Dutch rule, but also from Communist domination. They had learned that "the real revolution is a spiritual one" and that "the great conquest is to gain dominion, not over someone else, but over one's own self-centered materialism" (Babbitt 1975, 10-11).

Mental ills are legion today. They often spring from self-focus—thought turning so inward to the self that it loses balance or perspective. Whether termed neurosis or psychosis, dementia or depression, phobia or schizophrenia, or whether manifest as extreme nervousness and stress, as emotional imbalance, self-will and self-pity, as age-related lapses in memory or capacity, or as either inherited or acquired addictive/compulsive tendencies, such ills clearly illustrate that mentality constitutes and governs body and experience.

While genetic deficiencies, brain dysfunction, chemical imbalance, or trauma-induced abnormalcies account for some cases, more mental disorders relate to the self-assertion of a material ego or human will. Healing comes in the degree that human will is relinquished, balance is restored, and paralyzing fears or other fragmenting, destructive emotions, delusions, and reactions yield to more normal attitudes. Unfailing compassion, unvarying patience, and spiritually-based calm and assurance are requisite to break the torments of mental illness and restore one's true individuality.

People use both mental and physical ills to "escape" their environments. Reasons for this escape vary, but they can include: extreme disappointment or hurt, inability to cope, unwillingness to take responsibility, fear of failure, sometimes sheer boredom or selfishness. There is a choice to be made—consciously or unconsciously, and many seem unwilling or unable to make that choice.

That raises the question: can someone be helped who doesn't want to be helped? If an individual clings to a problem because it brings him attention or sympathy or support, or gives him an excuse, or (as with an addiction) gives him an illusion of ease or delays his having to face and master what he dreads, then is healing possible?

It was for the man at the pool of Bethesda. Those in Jesus' day possessed with "demons" or "evil spirits" often resisted the transforming Christ. "What have (we) to do with thee?" (Mark 5:6-9) was their cry. Yet, with the divine authority to which he was obedient and the divine Love with which he was imbued, Jesus cast out the evil possessing the individual. His charge to his followers was: "Heal the sick (those suffering inwardly and outwardly), cleanse the lepers (those morally and physically contaminated or outcast), raise the dead (those buried above ground, deadened to life and its meaning), cast out devils (personified evil): freely ye have received, freely give" (Matt.10:8).

In fact, all discord is a type of insanity—an inducement to believe that what is neither God-created nor sanctioned is both real and powerful. Severe ills would take over the individual, rob him of his true selfhood, totally absorb his thinking, and often dominate entire families, dictating everyone's actions, diminishing everyone's freedom.

In the same way, today's severe social, governmental, and economic problems often seem so pervasive, so complex and ingrained, so unsolvable, that people are tempted to feel helplessly bound, despairing of change, and so tend to withdraw, to become self-absorbed.

But even one individual can make a difference—can diffuse hatred or advance justice. One life can be a leaven, a catalyst for change or transformation in a community or situation. One individual experience of healing, one example of selflessness and courage, can bless and inspire in ever-widening circles.

Such is the case with Barbara Cummiskey, whose dramatic healing of multiple sclerosis was shared in an article/testimony entitled "The Miracle Day" in Guideposts (April, 1985, 1-5). In 1965, Barbara was an active teenager involved with gymnastics, her high school orchestra, an after school job, and her church's youth group. By 1978, she was in a wheelchair, feet and hands curled and useless, dependent on a constant supply of oxygen. She had been diagnosed in 1970. Medically, nothing could be done to stop the deterioration.

Her condition worsened. By 1980, a lung had collapsed, and she could barely see. To assist her breathing, a tracheostomy had been performed. Several years before, her pastor had given Barbara a goal: to grow in faith. Now she determined that her activity could be prayer—prayer for others. Then came June 7, 1981, her sister's birthday. Barbara did her best to make the needed effort to participate.

Two friends arrived. As they were visiting with Barbara, she heard a fourth voice. It was firm, audible, compelling. It said: "My child, get up and walk." Barbara complied. She writes: "This wasn't possible, of course—there were 1,001 medical reasons why this couldn't be happening. Yet there I stood, firmly, solidly, feeling tingly all over... I could breathe freely. And I could see... My hands were normal, not curled to my wrists. The muscles in my arms and legs were filled out whole."

Barbara headed toward the doorway. Family and friends crowded around her and jubilantly praised God. Her testimony concludes: "I don't know why God healed me... I only know that on (that) morning, I felt good about myself—mentally, emotionally and spiritually well. Through my prayer life, I was a busy, active member of the human family—not running or jumping or even walking like most people, but not separated from them by bitterness, self-pity, or despair. My mind and spirit were healthy and whole. And then God made my body whole too."

Questions we all have to answer in light of such an event include: Is such a restoration miraculous, or are there repeatable, provable, spiritual laws involved? Does God work in random, unpredictable, incomprehensible ways or naturally, expectably, reliably? Is there an "alternative" or ultimate reality of which we can all become aware and which has power to transform the human circumstance? What is the role of faith, of prayer, of spiritual understanding in maintaining wholeness or health? If matter is, as Einstein defines it, a "construction of the consciousness, an edifice of conventional symbols shaped by the senses of man" (Barnett 1948, 11), then aren't we dealing primarily with mental rather than physical factors in healing—whether that healing is of an individual, or of the nations? If so, then may it not be counterproductive to treat only symptoms? Is there a divine Will or Law that unmistakably regulates and governs human experience, conforming it to the divine purpose and to what is spiritually real?

Answers to such questions certainly proceed from faith—but from faith that is more than blind belief. Answers must proceed from an understanding of the actual nature of Creator and creation. Today people take for granted that they can fly globally. Astronauts land on the moon or rendezvous in space. The laws of aerodynamics have always existed. Access to or utilization of these laws only awaited mankind's readiness to comprehend them. Once discovered and proved, they haven't had to be pioneered again and again.

Similarly, once transcending spiritual laws are discovered, proved, and understood, they will transform human experience as they have done repeatedly over the centuries in the lives of many individuals. This discovery will take place as thought becomes receptive, not just individually but also globally, and there will be "healing of the nations" (Rev. 22:2).

What is the freedom mankind so ardently pursues? Isn't it freedom from ignorance, from fear and its limitations, from mistake and failure, from the oppression of false beliefs and systems of thought, from a lack of meaning, of value or worth? But this freedom can't be sheer license or total unrestraint. Can there really be self-government or self-determination except in obedience to God's government? Is there any freedom to be and do wrong or only freedom in being and doing right?

Ends never can justify means. If our means aren't right, then the end we hope to achieve never can be. One can never benefit himself by harming another. The self-forgetful love and spiritual perspective that fosters forgiveness, dispels fear, and sustains wholeness is the greatest healing agent of all.

Healing, however, can't simply be equated with restored physicality or better matter. That's why humility is essential. We can't use God or spiritual Truth to accomplish our own ends. But we can use whatever challenge arises to glorify God, to serve the divine purpose, and to be inwardly transformed.

Individuals who encounter severe trials are often tempted to ask: Why me? Jesus' own response in his hour of agony was: "To this end was I born, and for this cause came I into the world, that I should bear witness unto the truth..." (John 18:37). We learn that, while we may have no choice or voice in determining events, we can always choose how to view these events and how to deal with their consequences. The important thing is not what we expect out of life, but what Life (God) demands of us.

Despite much evidence to the contrary, we always have power to think rightly. Animal magnetism, the term Christian Scientists use for the mesmeric pull of wrong or matter-based thinking, would argue otherwise. The only "mind" anyone can lose is the belief in a limited, human personality or mentality. Because we reflect or express the one infinite Mind that is God, we have inherent power to hold our thoughts to good—both to what is spiritually and eternally valid or real and to what is humanly nearest right as God gives us to see that right.

There is a dimension beyond the human, however tragic. There is a divine plan and purpose that is good. We can learn to trust that purpose. It isn't doing nothing but is doing much and doing the best we can to yield to God's disposal of events, to understand and obey the divine Will or Law and to challenge whatever is at enmity with it. Robert Browning puts it well: "On earth the broken arcs, in heaven a perfect round."

There is never a time or circumstance when we can't put our weight in the scale with the eternal Right and live purposefully in accord with that Right—both in appreciation and love for all that is good, beautiful, and true and in opposition to whatever is ugly, hurtful, and false. Moreover, we can never be without the hope of eternal Life or unfailing Love. So thinking and doing, our lives will be our message, and that message will be heard and will bear fruit.

Chapter Six

CURRENT LITERATURE

"For precept must be upon precept...line upon line"
(Isa.28:10)

In Aesop's familiar fable of the six blind men and the elephant, each of the men tries to identify what he is touching and so define an elephant. One touches the elephant's leg and concludes that an elephant is like a tree trunk, and so on. All of them are right within the limited parameters of their perception and experience. But none of them grasp what an elephant really is. This serves, does it not, as an apt metaphor of mankind's search for ultimate Truth?

It is also an echo of Paul's "seeing through a glass darkly," or of the man blind from birth whose sight was restored by Jesus. When questioned and rebuked by the Pharisees, the man replied: "...one thing I know, that, whereas I was blind, now I see" (John 9:25).

One might ask: how can six blind men (or those who have grasped only a partial and imperfect sense of what actually exists) ever glimpse or comprehend Truth? They can learn from others' experiences or heed others' lessons, or they can have their own direct and definitive experience— something that of itself transforms their limited perspectives.

Much current literature—and there has been an explosion of shared perspectives in the self-help, abuse, health and recovery fields over the past decade—seems to provide some information, all valid, and some viewpoints, all legitimate, within the parameters of those authors' experiences, related to wholeness and healing, but not a complete or definitive grasp of the subject.

Humanity is not yet seeing "face to face." But there is growing light on the nature of health or wholeness and the fact that healing or recovery encompasses far more and extends far beyond medical technology or material means, however advanced.

Healing And The Mind

The 1993 PBS series conducted by respected journalist Bill Moyers, who is also a former White House Press Secretary and an ordained Baptist minister, and its companion volume both entitled: Healing and the Mind is a case in point. Perspectives from a number of eminent professionals in the health care field world-wide yielded interesting vignettes or aphorisms and pointed out current trends but did not provide the total picture.

Here are some examples gleaned from the series: Whatever you believe will benefit you will do so. Find your center and you will be healed. The mind is the body, but mind is more than brain. Every thought counts in the sense that moods, attitudes, emotions transform themselves into physical health or sickness. If you can learn to be comfortable in the midst of pain, it will disappear. You gain by what you give to others. Technology gets in the way of the mind/body relationship—there are a lot of things technology can't do. Disease can become an idolatry, or an excuse. Laughter, harmony, balance, peace are all components of health. Healing comes by evoking hope, and this is accomplished through love, not just a personal love, but the sense of an accepting, affirming Presence. There is a deep inner intelligence in every human being that knows what is needed for healing.

The series pointed to the fact that different cultures approach healing in vastly different ways. It presented convincing evidence for its conclusion: that thoughts and feelings, attitudes and beliefs, determine health. It explored answers to the fundamental questions: What is health, and what evokes or constitutes healing? But it failed to address more than indirectly the role of faith, prayer, or spirituality in healing. This omission seems the more glaring in light of its eventual definition of health as "self-acceptance," and of healing as a process of bringing forth wholeness or integrity in people—evoking their own inner resources.

Only those forms of alternative treatment deemed compatible with medical orthodoxy were investigated in the series. Yet, as one reviewer pointed out, "...implicit in all the information provided is an important challenge to the medical establishment's traditionally mechanistic approach to curing" (The Christian Science Monitor, 19 February, 1993, 13).

The final conversation of the series contained this comment from a doctor whose focus over the past twelve years has been on patients diagnosed with cancer: "Maybe there is no such thing as 'not being.' Maybe in some way we do go on... I think that healing happens only in the context of our imminent awareness of something larger than ourselves... I don't believe that we're alone. We are such a gift, each of us, to each other..." (Moyers 1993, 363).

Healing Words

Far more forthright is Dr. Larry Dossey's presentation in his recent book of the power of prayer to heal. Citing more than 130 studies done during the past 30 years, he insists that prayer is an important, scientifically verifiable factor in healing. In many of the studies, the beneficial effects were the same whether prayer was performed on site or at a distance. Dossey also makes a strong case for the influence of a doctor's beliefs and attitudes on his patients' health.

As for how one prays, Dossey refutes any formula or stereotyped pattern, indicating that prayer varies with personality types. He does imply that more effective than asking for or even willing or "imaging" a specific outcome is the prayer that yields to the divine Will and conforms human consciousness to a universal divine Intelligence and Love. Prayer, he concludes "says something incalculably important about who we are and what our destiny may be" (1993, 6).

Also important is his observation that one praying for another doesn't consider himself or herself to be the source of healing but only a conduit "through which healing flows from a higher power." He seems to indicate that prayer is a process of connecting with who we really are—an indication that "something about us is immortal or eternal."

Interestingly, Dossey explores, as do few other authors in this rapidly expanding field, the question of "black" or "negative" prayer—whether or not it has an effect. The answer lies in what one believes and how prayer is viewed. If intercessory, specific, or directed prayer is seen as mere thought-transference or one mind influencing another by means of suggestion, then negative as well as positive effects would be logical. Curses, spells, anathemas, personal manipulation, even death-wishes would be possible, and the medium through which such evils could most effectively operate would be fear or guilt. But if prayer is a means of glimpsing or experiencing the Divine or spiritually real, then it cannot be misused or become a tool for personal control. Such prayer can only bless since God is only and totally good.

Dossey tends to resist what he calls the "New Age" notion that one induces or is responsible for his own ills. In his analysis of prayer there is little discussion of self-examination or purification, of moral regeneration or spiritual transformation. Nor is there any significant reference to Biblical healing, perhaps because he sees himself as a physician not wanting to trespass on theology or spiritual teaching, or perhaps because he has embraced Buddhism. Still, he insists that the gap or distinction between the scientific and the spiritual is increasingly artificial.

Noting that the body of evidence for spiritual healing is often ignored because it doesn't fit well with prevailing secular ideas, Dossey concludes in his introduction that "Skirting the spiritual has had a shattering effect on every dimension of contemporary existence." He links many medically labelled and too-frequently ignored "spontaneous remissions" of serious ills with prayer or faith.

Dossey's sequel, Prayer is Good Medicine, is a kind of handbook for those who want to utilize prayer in conjunction with medical methods. In it, his advice to the sick is: "Use what works" (1996, 5). Unfortunately, he himself skirts the deeper questions of why prayer works, especially when medicine fails, or what enables spiritual healing to be more than mystical and random and to be measurable, predictable, and reproducible.

Remarkable Recovery

The link between healing regarded medically as spontaneous and faith is made emphatically by Caryle Hirshberg and Marc Ian Barasch in their recently published study of extraordinary healings—that is, healings that occur despite medical expectation or prognosis to the contrary. Like Dossey, these authors find that prayer works, but neither he nor they really answer how prayer operates or why it appears effective in some cases and not in others. They all concur that prayer has a placebo role. One's belief in the power of prayer (or of any therapy) they say has a great deal to do with the results.

In the Foreword to this study written by Larry Dossey, he comments: "Our (the medical profession's) collective neglect of remarkable recoveries is astonishing and utterly irrational" (1995, xii). He not only faults a fatalistic mentality among medical practitioners, but suggests that this negative mind-set—the "worst-scenario" approach—has damaging effects on patients. He concludes that "psychospiritual" influences figure dramatically in the many healing accounts explored by the authors.

Remarkable Recovery is a thorough exploration of long-neglected and deliberately disdained medical anomalies. At the outset, the authors reject the medical term: "spontaneous remission" since it suggests something temporary or something happening without a cause. They also take the medical profession to task for its self-serving dismissal of accounts of remarkable healings as merely "anecdotal," and suggest instead that these be regarded as "case histories" with important truths to reveal.

The detailed cases reviewed in this book, they contend, indicate there is an inner "healing system" present within each individual. There are also patterns apparent in many of the cases that suggest numerous psychological, social, and spiritual factors are involved either in addition to or in spite of what they call the "relentless biology" of illness.

The authors write: "The further we explored remarkable recovery, the more it seemed that belief— whether in a treatment, a person, a setting, or a system— was a key variable in what we began to think of as a mind-body-spirit equation" (1995, 102). In Chapter Five entitled: "In Search of the Miraculous," they investigate several phenomenal healings documented at Lourdes, and then share a number of other personal accounts of healings linked to Catholicism. They refer to this comment by Dr. Roger Pilon, the current medical director at Lourdes, that "at the heart of a cure...is the relationship with this God who is Love" (1995, 143). They then question whether it's possible to ever fully understand the mechanisms of "miracle" healing.

But in subsequent chapters they go beyond the notion of healing as miraculous to conclude that many diseases represent peculiar "refractions of personality" and that healing involves change, namely "becoming true," or putting off quirks of human disposition or personality in order to become "whole." Most survivors they found to be flexible, adaptable, resilient, willing to make the essential and positive choices needful for healing.

Investigating death-camp or prisoner-of-war survivors, they note that even helpless victims of hopeless situations may rise above themselves, and by so doing change themselves and others. They find a strong link between survival and immunity—a resistance now known to be modulated by "mind-body factors of psychoneuroimmunology." They quote one Auschwitz survivor who insisted that "only with forgiveness comes freedom." They conclude that a resolve to live meaningfully, a "differential focus on the good," a rich inner life, and, above all, connection—with one's authentic self, with others, and with God—are the underlying determinants of survival.

Struggling to define what they feel underlies remarkable recovery, the authors suggest that the key "healing system" is our genuine selfhood, mediated by a flow of information springing from the biological, mental, emotional, and spiritual life of every individual. This inner truth, they suggest, reveals itself to each of us in ways we can comprehend, often, but not always, in a context of some challenge or crisis.

Despite the authors' extensive investigation into the complexities of recovery in each of their cited cases, there is little attention given to factors which relate to the onset of disease. Other than the suggestion that there is a "recovery-prone personality" they avoid asking whether there are also disease-prone attitudes or to what extent disease is caused mentally. All of us can agree that prevention or the prophylactic art is higher and of greater importance than cure or therapeutic practices.

Like the Moyer series, the authors remain determinedly within the realm of contemporary medicine, even though their conclusions, and some of the cases they share, take them far beyond that realm. Only by implication is there a hint that healings which seem on the surface to be highly random and unexplainable may represent a higher law or alternative reality at work.

Barasch and Hirshberg do not mention current views of physical scientists, especially quantum theorists regarding the nature of matter and "observer-created" reality. They do censure many medical prognoses as "self-fulfilling prophecies" and indicate that the key to healing lies within each individual and the individual's own views, attitudes, approaches, and choices.

The Sacred Self

Thomas Csordas, Associate Professor of Anthropology at Case Western University, in his scholarly study of charismatic healing, deals primarily with the phenomenology of self and self-transformation. Csordas' focus is on Catholic Charismatic Renewal, a movement that incorporates Pentecostal practices into traditional Catholicism. His thesis is that Charismatic (or, by implication, spiritual) healing is about the "self." To be healed is to experience one's sacred self.

Charismatic healing may incorporate or utilize ritual, but is not purely ritualistic. In many parts of the United States it is ecumenical in membership, rather than denominational. The author approaches his study from the standpoint of agnosticism—from the common anthropological presumption that religious healing works because it is like psychotherapy.

His argument is that the "locus of efficacy" in healing is not "symptoms, symbolic meanings, or social relationships, but the self in which all of these are encompassed" (1994, 3). The self processes he finds articulated in Charismatic healing are personal imagination, memory, language, and emotion.

Charismatic healing includes a repertoire of distinct acts or states, such as Divine Empowerment (the experiencing of divine power in various ways), Protection (by invoking religious figures, particularly Christ Jesus and the Virgin Mary, or by prayer), Revelation (derived from Scripture, prophecy, and vision), Deliverance (from ancestral bondage or evil spirits and beliefs), Sacramental Grace (by means of communion and reconciliation), and Emotional release (forgiveness).

Csordas suggests that the common effect of religious healing is not simply to remove a disease and its symptoms but to transform the meaning of the illness, and through it, to experience self-realization. He concludes that ritual healing operates on a "margin of disability"—that is, it challenges the person's commitment to a habitual posture of incapacity. Such healing is also characterized by an "incremental efficacy"—meaning steps toward healing rather than a sudden, total release; by the "elaboration of alternatives" or possibilities where before there had seemed none; and by the actualization of change.

For Charismatics, spiritual healing and spiritual growth or transformation are inseparable. Such phenomena as prostration in prayer, or being "slain in the Spirit" or "resting in the Spirit" indicate response to a divine presence and submission to divine power—getting one's self (ego) out of the way and yielding to God.

The "sacred" or "healed" self, then, becomes no "self" at all he declares, but represents surrender of the struggling human personality or will to one's eternal spiritual being—to the identity that is God created, constituted and governed. Perhaps this statement could be seen as analogous: "Self-renunciation of all that constitutes a so-called material man, and the acknowledgment and achievement of his spiritual identity as the child of God, is Science (divine law or purpose) that opens the very flood-gates of heaven; whence good flows into every avenue of being, cleansing mortals of all uncleanness, destroying all suffering, and demonstrating the true image and likeness" (Eddy 1896, 185).

Despite his agnosticism and perhaps inadvertently Csordas has touched upon the fundamental Christian concept of putting off "the old man" (the old, material concept of being) and putting on the new (the spiritual self), "which after God is created in righteousness and true holiness" (Eph.4:22-24).

The Uncommon Touch

Tom Harpur, Canada's leading writer on religious, spiritual, and ethical issues, and a former Anglican priest, has written a book that is illuminating and practical in its investigation of spiritual healing.

The book's title comes from the early Christian practice of laying on of hands—a practice used today in the resurgence of interest in spiritual healing in many main-line churches. Harpur employs the term as a metaphor for a variety of non-medical approaches to healing, most of them religious in nature. In fact, he stresses in Chapter Three entitled "The Religious Roots of Healing," that "Throughout history, healing has held a primary place in religions around the world" (1994, 38). Theologically, he states, "healing (in its broadest sense) is what God is all about."

He takes the position that healing may well hold the key "to the renewal of religion, and, more importantly, of spirituality, in the...world of the future." He considers healing to be that direct experience of divine power that can unite spiritually devout people of diverse backgrounds and traditions. He also sees healing as bridging and finally closing the gap that has existed between the sciences and religion.

In the Chapter on Prayer, he indicates that prayer puts one in touch with an ultimate truth or larger reality, and can thus be considered "scientific." Although he accepts that resistance or opposition to a healer (or to spiritual means) can sometimes block healing, he considers that healing follows specific laws and is therefore, not always conditional on mere faith or belief.

As a minister, Harpur participated in a number of healing services and observed tangible results. He insists that quackery or charlatanism—particularly among the television evangelists—while it has turned many observers away from serious investigation of spiritual means in healing, cannot discredit the genuine transformation or in-breaking of spiritual reality that constitutes true healing. He also concludes that most authentic healers have passed through some "Calvary of illness" or affliction of their own in order to become "wounded healers" of others.

Although his research has dealt largely with those who regard non-medical healing as complementary to and not a substitute for conventional medical practice, he details serious and perhaps fatal problems within the modern medical establishment, particularly with regard to care of the elderly, who are "overdoctored, overmedicated, and overhospitalized." He considers the effort to prolong physical existence medically to have created a funding nightmare capable of bankrupting Canada's national economy. His criticism of the "tunnel vision of the biomedical model" which too often strips the patient "not just of dignity but of...full humanity" is sharp.

He also admits that, while there is widespread dissatisfaction with Western medicine today, the medical establishment itself "takes a very dismissive or patronizing" if not actually hostile attitude toward any other approach. The fact is, there is plenty of "hard evidence" for the reliability and success of spiritual healing. Resistance is understandable, Harpur says, since paradigms change slowly, and since there has been tremendous long-term investment in medical technology and an allopathic approach.

Harpur takes the position that ultimately all healing is self-healing. Not that one heals himself, but that one's sense of himself is what needs healing, and the resources for this healing lie within each of us and are fundamentally spiritual in nature. Disease itself may be a cry for help or a need for change. Disease often compels a reshaping and redefining of values, an awakening to ultimate meaning or destiny. What matters are the choices we make, and the courage, faith, and hope with which we make them, and this conclusion applies to the resolving, not just of individual, but of societal ills as well.

Can we not all conclude, as Harpur does, that "however deep the valley of the shadow through which we or others may be passing, the Ultimate Ground of the universe is with us all?" Because "the everlasting arms" are always underneath (Deut.33:27), all is and must be well.

Other Seminal Literature

The "gurus" of the mind/body movement—all of
them successful, widely read authors—include the late
Norman Cousins, Dr. Joan Borysenko, and Surgeon Bernie
Siegel. Also influential are Dr. Deepak Chopra, a former
hospital chief of staff and President of the American
Association for Ayurvedic Medicine; Psychiatrist M.
Scott Peck whose concern with spirituality and candid discussion
of love and its risks propelled his first book into stellar status
with more than seven million copies sold; and Dr. Elizabeth
Kubler-Ross whose reflections on death and dying, as well
as study of near-death experiences have interested many.

In addition to such literature, there is a growing list
of authors, including journalists, sharply critical of the
medical establishment and its reductionist approach. An
example is a book by Charles Inlander, Lowell Levin and
Ed Weiner entitled: Medicine on Trial published in 1988
which details an appalling story of ineptitude, malfeasance,
neglect, and arrogance in modern medical practice. More
than an exposé, the book also offers a prescription for change.

Ivan Illich, in Medical Nemesis, takes the position
that the medical establishment has become a threat to health.
He substantiates this position with a devastating analysis of
"iatrogenesis" (doctor-created illness). He concludes that the
society which can reduce professional intervention to a
minimum will best support individual autonomy (and
responsibility) and provide the best conditions for health.

Journalist Lynn Payer, argues that medical
professionals, drug companies, insurers, and others who
profit from making people believe they are sick are Disease
Mongers. She singles out unnecessary surgery, excessive

testing, drug company profits, and the cholesterol scam as particular offenders. A practising physician, Dr. Robert Mendelsohn first published his Confessions of a Medical Heretic in 1979. He states flatly: "I believe that more than ninety percent of Modern Medicine could disappear from the face of the earth—doctors, hospitals, drugs, and equipment—and the effect on our health would be immediate and beneficial" (14).

Add to the above categories a third: the explosion of books about healing—not medical, but mental, emotional, relational, inspirational. Some of these offerings grow from personal experience; some, from professional practice. A number of these books are by ministers, healers, pastoral counselors. What they indicate is a tremendous need, interest, and awakening in the entire field of health or wellness, as well as a strong trend toward alternative methods, particularly spiritual and psychospiritual.

Many works are outgrowths of particular ills or needs, such as: compulsive/addictive behaviors and programs (especially 12-step programs) to change those behaviors; violence and dysfunction in families, including co-dependence; stress-induced ills; even dietary "discoveries" relating not only to proper weight maintenance, but to prevention and healing of various diseases. Many books speak of "inner" healing, of cleansing of memories, of the importance of forgiveness and love on the one hand, or of the negative effects of depression, anger, and fear on the other.

Someone entering a major bookstore for the first time might conclude that Americans in general are obsessed with health and healing. The fact remains that the plethora of such published writings indicate a growing recognition

Healing

that health in general relates to far more than bodily or physical well-being.

Health has to do with wholeness, with self-acceptance and transcendence, with living lovingly and meaningfully, with being genuine, and with the absolute necessity of purity or integrity, of harmony, order, balance, and meaning—all spiritual states. As yet, too few authors— or too few whose works have been recognized in major bookstores—have dealt definitively with the link between spirituality and health, but the list is growing.

Victims No Longer

The strongest challenge to self-perpetuation of the attitudes, behaviors, and memories that constitute the "mind-set" of victimization comes, not out of the most recent mind/ body literature nor even from those who have explored alternative methods of healing, but from those writers who have forthrightly exposed abuse—particularly sexual abuse of children—in our society. Most of their writings have been published within the past decade.

Their exploration of the extent of such abuse and its prolonged effects, as well as their efforts to provide healing solutions, have enhanced recognition of the necessity for inner change. Uniformly, they have challenged the notion of incurability, or of the impossibility of recovery from the resulting trauma.

They also agree that healing begins with breaking the silence or uncovering the wound that has often festered for years, and that has affected not just the survivor but all those close to that survivor. They tend to regard this uncovering as difficult and painful, requiring courage, patience, support, and a willingness to challenge ingrained perspectives.

Some writers have focused on Christianity's role in fostering this abuse, and on the damaging effects of such abuse on the development of a healthy spirituality or God-concept (see Brown and Bohn 1989; Cashman 1993; Doehring 1993; Gudorf 1992; and Imbens and Jonker 1992).

Certainly, the primary consequence of sexual abuse has been its impairment of a healthy self-concept for the abused, and the subsequent development of coping behaviors or attitudes that often lead to abnormalcy and disease. The collateral damage such abuse does to families is immense.

Even less acknowledged and written about than sexual abuse of young girls has been exploitation and misuse of boys and the often life-long perpetuation of consequences of such abuse. Mike Lew, in his influential study of men recovering from incest and other childhood abuse entitled Victims No Longer, gives this simple but fundamental definition of recovery: "Recovery is the freedom to make choices in your life that aren't determined by the abuse" (1988, xviii).

Most of these writers are concerned with such freedom: freedom to be oneself; freedom from the ghosts of the past; freedom from attitudes and behaviors that are self-defeating; freedom even from theological doctrines that encourage self-depreciation and foster fear, guilt and shame, and from psychological teachings and secular views that label and oppress.

In the introduction to The Courage to Heal, Ellen Bass and Laura Davis insist that healing of victimization is possible—not merely the alleviation of symptoms for survivors or their ability to function adequately, but the possibility of actually thriving, based on a sense of wholeness, satisfaction in life, and genuine trust and love. They also insist that such deep healing doesn't happen unless the wounded individual consciously chooses it (1988, 20).

Sexual Assault and Abuse, a handbook for clergy and religious professionals first published in 1987, has been important to many who seek to respond in a compassionate, healing way to victims of violence and abuse. The handbook grew out of a series of workshops on sexual violence held in 1984 for clergy, when the best-known material available in book form was Marie Fortune's Sexual Violence, The Unmentionable Sin. The handbook's editors point out that theological questions and practical responses—both to victims and to trauma—are thoroughly intertwined. They admit to gaps or inadequacies in the work: silence on the question of male victims; on the effect of pornographic materials and the larger influence of media sensualism and violence; on treatment for perpetrators or offenders; and on the fact that ritual confession and absolution cannot substitute for reformation and rehabilitation.

Several writers have focused on incest in particular (see E. Sue Blume 1990; Susan Forward and Craig Buck 1978; and Diana Russell 1986). Leonard Shengold's study of the effects of childhood abuse and deprivation: Soul Murder has been an influential resource-book for therapists, as has Judith Herman's Trauma and Recovery.

In Confronting the Victim Role, Barry and Emily McCarthy write: "Ideally, every child deserves to grow up in a safe, secure, loving, nurturing family, with no abuse or dysfunction. However, the perfect, problem-free, totally loving childhood is not the reality for any child... Growing up in a healthy family includes experiencing frustrations and disappointments" (1993, 12).

They take special exception to the prevailing "catharsis" theory that advocates the expression of feelings of hurt, frustration and anger, insisting that such negative reactions tend to feed on themselves. Still, they acknowledge such feelings can't remain hidden but must be dealt with and transformed into positive goals. Fundamentally, they advocate living in the present and refusing to be controlled by trauma of the past.

Few could disagree. While the McCarthys assert that the important preparation of childhood is learning to live as an independent, responsible, loving, and self-sufficient adult, they offer few guidelines for such an important achievement. My own hope for childhood experiences—even those most difficult to grow beyond—is that they ultimately promote a sense of oneself as spiritual, cherished by and inseparable from an unfailing divine Love, and imbued with a sense of self-worth, meaning and purpose.

Consensus

What are some of the commonalities emerging in all this literature? 1) that mind (thought, belief, emotion) not only affects body; thought constitutes body and experience; 2) that the individual is more than simply a bio-chemical organism; 3) that inherent in each individual is a natural immunity as well as a healing "system" or capacity, and these are fundamentally mental and spiritual; 4) that while belief or faith is an important factor in the efficacy of any healing method, non-medical healing isn't limited to faith, since it relates to an alternative reality and to the utilization of spiritual laws; 5) that we each have responsibility for our own health; 6) that while we can't always govern circumstances, we can govern our response to these circumstances and so determine whether we will be victims or not; 7) that through prayer or a sense of connectedness to the Divine, people are renewed and restored mentally, physically, and spiritually.

While there is one ultimate Truth, there are many different ways or paths, as well as stages, of arriving at this Truth. Unity or consensus cannot be imposed from without. Agreement or a shared perspective becomes possible only as individuals share common experiences, walk common paths, and join in similar purposes and values. Ultimately, unity must rest on recognition of a common Creator, an originating divine Intelligence and Benevolence, establishing the dignity and worth of every individual, and on each individual's response to that Creator's laws or demands.

The fact remains, as Surgeon Bernie Siegel avers, that love heals. Disease of whatever sort is ultimately related to a sense of brokenness, discord, loss of ease, wholeness, and peace. Lasting ease and peace come finally from feeling at one with the Infinite. As Tom Harpur puts it: "No greater therapy exists in all the world than the consciousness of life...as something ultimately in the control of an infinitely loving mind and presence" (Harpur 1994, 72).

When "bad things happen to good people" (to borrow Rabbi Harold Kushner's phrase), and they frequently do, what can we conclude? We conclude that the Love that created and sustains the universe will set things right, will adjust or correct, restore or renew, as needed, inasmuch as the spiritual always governs the outward. In the process, we will grow spiritually. The lessons we learn we can then illuminate for others.

Is humanity, then, at a point where it can arrive, if not at unity or absolute oneness of thought with regard to the origins of ill-health, or even the most successful methods of effecting healing or facilitating recovery, at least at the intimate relationship between physical or mental health and spiritual wholeness? Will the costly failures of merely material approaches and the ultimate meaninglessness of secularism bring people together in the direction of genuine spirituality? Not mysticism and otherworldliness, not religiosity and denominationalism, but genuine godliness and reverence for creation can answer humanity's deepest needs.

Have we reached a point where more of those who have experienced tragedy, who have felt victimized, who have struggled with injustice and despair, begin to awaken to the "self-healing" that is always possible? Will many who have been "seeing through a glass darkly" begin to see "face to face," or who have known only in part begin to know as they are known of God? (I Cor.13:12) There are encouraging indications that more are reaching this point.

Whatever the spiritual fact or law, the human sense of things must ultimately conform to it. God's will must be done on earth as it is in heaven. Spiritual healing is that direct experience of the Divine that transforms human thought and experience. It is God, Spirit, glimpsed or understood. It is the Word (God's message or revelation to humanity) "made flesh"—made practical. It is the human sense of things coinciding with the divinely real.

This is the saving Truth or Christ that Jesus exemplified. He was imbued with the Holy Spirit, which anointed and empowered him to do the works he did and to reveal spiritual reality to humanity. This Truth is the ultimate "way" or Savior from ignorance and untruth. Other prophets or spiritual seers both before and after Jesus' advent have manifested the Christ to some degree. Jesus was the highest manifestation of the Christ, the consummate example of divinity's embrace of humanity. He lived what he taught, hence Christliness or genuine spirituality is the only foundation on which lasting healing (transformation of mind, soul, body) can be accomplished.

Theologians of many traditions are approaching consensus today—are uniting on the need for religion to be experiential and vital. God, they've come to feel, must be relevant, demonstrable; Truth must be impartial, universal. The Spirit and its power must be imminent as well as transcendant. God's gifts and promises must be felt, realized, and fulfilled.

In fact, there has been tremendous leavening or change not just in theology, but in the physical sciences and in medicine, as well as psychology. These disciplines, often divergent and at variance, are coming together in their search for truth. There remain strong areas of disagreement: over a view of evil and how best to deal with it; over matter as substance; over the nature of being as fundamentally biological and material or spiritual. Change always evokes reaction from entrenched viewpoints, but the evolution taking place in human thinking can't be stopped.

The great challenge of some prophetic insight is to be in the world so as to speak understandably to the world, but still not be of the world. It is to retain the integrity or purity of the revelation, since adulterating truth destroys its vitality and efficacy, while still communicating it effectively to others. The wonder of every experience of spiritual healing is that it attests the validity and authority of what is real and true. It also brings continual spiritual renewal—a return to and enhancement of the original vision.

The gradual enlightenment and progress of past decades can't be reversed. Humanity doesn't need to "till the soil"—to keep going over and over the same ground, relearning again and again the same hard lessons. Today's fresher perspectives are available, and with the help of technology can be communicated and utilized worldwide.

Most of us can agree with Scott Peck that "life is difficult." The human experience isn't a playground—it isn't intended for leisure and entertainment. Our present experience is a classroom—a preparatory learning experience that can be a joyous adventure, full of beauty and meaning, of continual possibilities and limitless opportunities. The purpose of this classroom is to awaken us to spiritual reality. This reality is Life eternal.

What we call death is not a finality, a termination of life, joy, affection, hope. It is a transition, a going on, a further learning. This passing or transition need not be difficult, prolonged, painful—any more than birth need be so. For those who have utilized well the present experience, there will be blessings and rewards hereafter, and always further unfoldment. If death comes abruptly or in a cruel and untimely way, there is the sure comfort of knowing that a loved one can never be separated from divine Love—that one's true spiritual selfhood remains forever intact. Death is not the experience of the one who goes on, but of those who remain.

Jesus' promise was: "If a man keep my saying (if he adheres to the truth I have taught), he shall never see (be impressed with the picture of or deceived by) death" (John 8:51).

What's important is that we make the most of every present opportunity—that we, by our examples and our own hard-won lessons, help one another and learn more of the meaning of Love. By our own proofs, we can illumine each other's paths. We can share insights. We can patiently encourage, tenderly support and care. But we can't walk for another or even rightly compare one person's progress with another's. Salvation is both individual and inevitable, and healing, both bodily and spiritually, is in its fullest sense what it means to be saved.

Chapter Seven

CONCLUSION

"Behold, I make all things new." (Rev. 21:5)

Rejoicing In Tribulation

Paul knew about victimization. He was a perpetrator of abuse, and then suffered much persecution himself. Through affliction he learned that "in all...things we are more than conquerors through him that loved us" (Rom.8:37). "When I am weak" (least able of myself to do anything), he said, "then am I strong"—strong in reliance on a power beyond my own (II Cor.12:l0).

Paul wrote a great deal about glorying or rejoicing in tribulation—that sifting process through which the dross, the tares, the wrongs are separated out from the pure, the wheat, the right. He blessed God for comforting us in all our tribulation "that we may be able to comfort them which are in any trouble, by the comfort wherewith we ourselves are comforted of God" (II Cor.1:3-4).

Humanly speaking, everyone experiences this tribulation to some degree. Everyone encounters difficulties, hurts, challenges, ills, failures, occasionally tragedy. Everyone makes mistakes. Not infrequently, the innocent suffer. Jesus' teaching was: "...it must needs be that offences come; but woe to that man by whom the offence cometh" (Matt.18:7).

The important thing is how we individually deal with such challenges. In our nation there has grown up a vast array of both private and governmental agencies to protect those that are vulnerable and to assist those in need. A wide range of helping professionals and a variety of methods of recovery that are constantly evolving are also available. For most people, there are family members, neighbors, friends, fellow workers or church members that provide practical loving support and a kind of safety net.

This is all good to the extent that it represents temporary aid. But such assistance helps not at all if it induces dependency on others, or encourages the notion that wrong attitudes and behaviors have no consequence, or that health and well-being are fundamentally material.

When one is in pain or is hurting, physical relief or emotional comfort becomes paramount. But the pursuit of physical well-being can't become God. It is a fundamental mistake—a reversal—when worship of a physical body and efforts to preserve a material existence take priority over spiritual demands and purposes.

Life has to be God-centered, not self or body centered. In fact, well-being that is manifest outwardly and is neither uncertain nor precarious must proceed from inner and spiritual health or wholeness. Therefore, the healing or transformation of thought that best advances individual and collective progress and that best meets humanity's needs proceeds from a reliance on God that is radical and a pursuit of spiritual understanding that is uncompromising.

Divine Love will always come to us where we are and meets our needs in ways we can understand, as Jesus showed when he got into the boat with his disciples, though he could have continued walking across the stormy sea (Mark 6:47-51), or when he provided food to the hungry multitude though he declared of himself: "I have meat to eat that ye know not of" (John 4:32).

However, use of material means of aid should be temporary, neither a life-long support system substituting for one's own responsibility, nor an entitlement to neglect either one's own spiritual growth or human well-being. In fact, unless one is willing to help himself, at least to some extent, others' efforts on his behalf will amount to little more than caretaking.

In the last analysis, redemption or healing comes from within each individual in response to a Power greater than oneself. The best help toward recovery will be whatever prompts repentance—the needed change of heart and perspective—and then awakens one to the spiritual reality that is always at hand.

Those who would foster such healing must often act humanly in terms of "what is nearest right under the circumstances" (Eddy 1896, 288), though it is seldom easy to know with certainty just what that may be. Readiness for a spiritual consciousness of being cannot be forced. But by holding steadfastly to the spiritual counterfact or alterative Truth, and listening humbly for divine guidance, both helpers and those needing help will be led of God, and by degrees the harmony, freedom, and dominion God bestows will be realized.

So, when trauma or harm is inflicted on us or on someone we love or want to help, what is our most effective response? Obviously, the wrong must be practically dealt with—it can't be concealed or ignored, but must be uncovered and, to the extent possible, rectified. We can pray to be like Ananias, an agent in helping one who is blinded to receive sight, to gain insight or spiritual discernment (Acts 9:17-18). Without a doubt, "...error, when found out is two-thirds destroyed, and the remaining third kills itself" (Eddy 1896, 210).

Because experience is always subjective, whatever improves thought will improve experience. But the healing that is transformational involves far more than simply restructuring human thinking or substituting positive for negative human thoughts. Instead, such healing necessitates the yielding of a human sense of things to the divine—to what God knows and purposes for each individual.

Even in the greatest tragedies, the comfort that is of God comes from glimpsing a transcendent reality, from the in-breaking of spiritual light. This light reveals that one's eternal, spiritual selfhood remains forever intact, inviolable, untouched by any inadvertent or intentional harm, even by the self-deluded evil that operates in the name of good.

The ability to see beyond the outward evidence or to judge "not according to the appearance" but righteously (John 7:24), is prophetic in nature. It recognizes that the spiritual fact governs and adjusts the outward or human circumstance. From this spiritual standpoint, one can be freed from the inner consequences of sharp disappointments, from the shame and shock of betrayals, from the terror of pain and harm, and can be helped to forgive.

Forgiveness doesn't pardon wrongdoing or set aside its consequences, since what one sows, he must inevitably reap. Only genuine repentance and reform can lift one out of the anguish and penalty of his own mistakes. Even moral idiocy must eventually yield to the discipline of prison and scaffold (Eddy 1906, 202).

Forgiveness frees the one who feels victimized from the corrosiveness of bitterness, anger, and resentment, and the hopelessness of depression, blame, and fear. "Hate no one;" writes Mrs. Eddy, "for hatred is a plague-spot that spreads its virus and kills at last... If you have been badly wronged, forgive and forget: God will recompense this wrong... Never return evil for evil..." (1896, 12).

The opposite of desecration is consecration; the opposite of loss is restoration; the opposite of contamination or corruption is purification. The opposite of death (of hope, trust, or affection) is renewal and rebirth. That's what spiritual healing is: the recapturing of one's original innocence, the renewal of inherent faith, hope, and joy; redemption from bondage to past hurts or self-destructive attitudes and behaviors; restoration of wasted years and fruitless efforts. Healing is evidence of divine Love's presence, activity, and victory.

Recovery from anything hurtful or damaging requires repentance (transformation of thought), reformation (changed attitudes and behavior), regeneration (renewal). It is God "making all things new" (Rev.21:5). Healing is the natural operation of God's will or law, understood. Almost a half-century ago, Agnes Sanford wrote: "Some day we will understand the principles that underlie the...powers of God, and we will accept (divine) intervention as simply and naturally as we do the radio and television... If one thinks of a (healing) miracle not as the breaking of God's laws but as (the) use (or operation of) His laws, then the world is full of miracles." She concludes: "God does nothing except by law" (Sanford 1947, 20). She also writes of healing as restoration of the soul—the selfhood—of the original person (Sanford 1966, 134).

The angel or blessing in any trauma is the opportunity it gives us to grow spiritually. We learn from what we suffer. Trials give us evidence of a higher law in operation. Through much tribulation, Paul taught, we "enter the kingdom"—we begin to recognize and experience God's reign within (Acts 14:22).

Whenever we take the position that some ill can only do us good, or lift us higher, we begin to be its master. By facing and conquering an injury or discord, we thereby become "wounded healers" to others. We are empowered to give others guidance, comfort and reassurance—to open their eyes and deepen their faith. In thus blessing others, we are blessed in return, and we discover the meaning and purpose of our lives.

Choice and Change

Do we, then, heal ourselves? Do we bring about our own recovery? No. What we do is choose to respond to ultimate Reality or transcendent Truth, to the Holy Spirit that is Love, and that alone awakens, inspires, and thereby heals. What is healed is our sense of ourselves as wounded, vulnerable, unworthy, mortal and hopelessly stuck in some problem or in some self-defeating pattern of behavior and response. Recovery means more than regaining what has been lost. It means seeing that, in reality, one's true spiritual status and wholeness can never be lost.

Healing requires openness to divine goodness, faith grounded in understanding of divine power. It involves the casting out of false gods, the yielding of human ego or will to the divine Will or Law.

We do not transform ourselves but respond to a transforming influence, in the same way that the outside atmosphere produces a change in a thermometer. We are essentially reflections of the Divine. Responding to that reality, we image its glory (Drummond 1893). As Paul puts it: "...we all, with open face beholding as in a glass the glory of the Lord, are changed into the same image...even as by the Spirit of the Lord" (II Cor.3:18).

Just as the leaf turns naturally to the light, we inevitably respond to and correspond with the "Spirit of the Lord" because we are inherently spiritual. That is our true or genuine nature. Such turning is hastened by our willingness to yield to that fact, and with humility and obedience conform our lives to it.

What answer will we give to Jesus' perennial question: "Wilt thou be made whole?" We may even paraphrase his question thus: Will you be what God has made you to be: whole, complete, perfect, sound in the divine image? Will you yield your sense of yourself (or, perhaps, others) as pitiful, wounded, disadvantaged, declining? Will you rise out of that false and demoralizing self-concept and assume your true status as a child of God? If we're ready to choose rightly, our answer will be Yes, and we'll experience healing.

When we can see ourselves rightly in God's image, then and only then can we see others rightly. That is what it means to love one's neighbor as oneself. Entrenched beliefs or self-concepts to the contrary are often stubborn, prideful, willful. The human ego fights for itself, often deliberately persisting in the very attitudes or behaviors that cause it the most harm. Then one becomes literally his own worst enemy, either destroying or reversing his own natural immunity to harm. Hence the necessity of becoming as a little child, willing to let go the old in order to put on the new (Eddy 1906, 323-324).

A helpful lecture entitled: "Can we change?" makes the point that surface or superficial changes—in roles, locations, jobs—are simply transference phenomena. But the change that is therapeutic involves insights or experiences that alter the course of our thoughts and lives, without ever changing the essential "me" that is spiritual and ongoing (Redfern 1975). Such healing change comes more frequently and easily as we pursue a quest for greater wisdom, spirituality, or fulfillment, and not simply seek physical cure or ease.

When our goal is to know and honor God, there can be no failure or disappointment—even under the most severe circumstances. In late 1979, Philip Newgent of St. Louis was involved in a serious accident. He had lost control of his car and been thrown out of it, remaining unconscious until found by the police. The hospital physician candidly told his wife that if her husband lived through the night, he would be a vegetable for the rest of his life.

Dire predictions continued for the next two weeks while Philip remained in a coma. The doctors suggested an operation to remove part of his brain, but his wife refused. After her earnest prayer all one night, coupled with a determination to acknowledge only God's control, the hospital staff moved Philip the next day from intensive care to a private room, although he was still paralyzed on one side and unable to talk. In another week, he was moved home with the assistance of a Christian Science visiting nurse.

There was no outlining by either husband or wife of when or how the healing might come, only a joyous anticipation of good. Within two months, Philip was driving again; and at the end of three months he was back at work. A medical examination confirmed his complete recovery.

The wife refers to the whole experience as "a lesson in knowing God's love." Philip's memory of the incident goes back only to the time when he returned home from the hospital, but the weeks, he says, were filled with "intense, radiant joy" (Testimony <u>Christian Science Sentinel</u> 20 December, 1993).

Gifts of the Spirit

It should be obvious that to receive the gifts of the Spirit, or to enjoy the fruits of the Spirit (love, joy, peace, longsuffering, gentleness, goodness, faith, meekness, temperance), we need to be spiritually-minded.

Spirituality has no denominational label. But the letter (mere ecclesiastical doctrine, formalism, dogma and ritual, or preaching without living godliness) lacks spiritual unction and vitality. Paul writes of diverse spiritual gifts: of wisdom and knowledge, faith, healing and the working of miracles, prophecy, discerning of spirits, tongues and their interpretation (I Cor.12:8-11). But he makes plain that the greatest of all these, and the most excellent way, is love—the kindness, charitableness, forgiveness that never fails (I Cor.13).

It is the Spirit that empowers and quickens. "I can do all things through Christ (the spirit of Truth and Love) which strengtheneth me," Paul declared (Phil.4:13). And so can we. Genuine spirituality infuses us with healing potency. It undergirds the conscious dominion with which we can detect, rebuke, and resist the mental impositions of discord and disease.

Spirituality also constitutes our best defense, enabling us to distinguish the voice, Word, or Spirit of God and its divine energy from the "spirits" or voices, the hypnotic messages or suggestions of the "carnal mind." It alerts us to those "false prophets that speak a vision of their own heart" (Jer.23:16). Genuine spirituality involuntarily repels animality and its mesmeric influence.

Spirituality lifts us above the currents of matter-based thinking. It focuses our attention, not on the temporal or the things that are seen, but on the eternal—not on what we (or others) seem to be but on what we really are. Because the "spiritual reality is the scientific fact in all things" (Eddy 1906, 207), and because spiritual reality determines human outcomes, the Spirit "helps our infirmities," and ultimately delivers humanity "from the bondage of corruption into the glorious liberty of the children of God" (Rom.8:21).

Prayer That Saves

Prayer or communion with God is the means by which spirituality is gained and maintained. To be effective prayer must be lived. In prayer, we don't ask Deity to change what the Infinite never made and would never sanction, but we open ourselves to a transforming Reality. The Psalmist prayed: "Open Thou mine eyes, that I may behold wondrous things out of Thy law" (Ps.119:18).

Prayer heals. We read in James: "Is any among you afflicted? Let him pray... Is any sick among you? Let him call for the elders of the church...and the prayer of faith shall save the sick, and the Lord shall raise him up... The effectual fervent prayer of a righteous man availeth much" (James 5:13-16).

To get out of ourselves (out of our common self-focused and earthbound perspectives) and into God to such an extent that healing becomes no longer power but divine grace is the essence of heartfelt communion with God or Truth. When we know Truth from the heart, it frees us from untruth—from accepting as valid or legitimate only that which is humanly supposed or imposed.

A consummate example of this is Marolyn Ford's account of her healing of total blindness. Soon after graduation from high school in 1960, Marolyn's sight began to fail. Nevertheless, with considerable courage and faith and despite what she describes as the emotional instability and psychological shock of her handicap, she enrolled in Tennessee Temple College. There she met and married Acie Ford, who became a Baptist minister. Their daughter was born in 1968, but by 1972, Marolyn had lost even peripheral vision and was forced to enroll in a three month program for the blind.

There she learned that her acceptance by others who were sighted depended solely on herself. She also learned that, despite her handicap, she was not a victim, and that God still had a purpose for her. She learned naturalness, confidence, courage, and gained freedom from self-consciousness in witnessing to God's ever-present help.

Many times during the ten years of their marriage, the couple would pray for healing, but it never came. Despite their acceptance of the continuing problem, Marolyn's blindness remained a burden. Late on the evening of August 25, 1972—Acie's birthday—they both cried as he prayed: "Oh God, You can restore Marolyn's eyesight tonight. I know You can do it! And, God, if it be Your will, I pray You will do it tonight."

Suddenly, Marolyn could see! They were overwhelmed with joy. For the first time, she could really see her husband, her daughter, their home. The next day, news of the healing spread quickly, and caution and disbelief were voiced by some. The following Sunday, Marolyn gave her testimony in church, and many wept unashamedly.

Days later, at Acie's insistence, Marolyn had her eyes examined. The doctor's startling report indicated that her eyes, medically speaking, were the same. In other words, from a physical standpoint, sight was not possible. But Marolyn's sight remained, and over the years she has spoken to many audiences about her experience (Ford 1975).

Her experience confirms the following: "Prayer means that we desire to walk and will walk in the light so far as we receive it, even though with bleeding footsteps, and that waiting patiently on the Lord, we will leave our real desires to be rewarded by Him... Self-forgetfulness, purity, and affection are constant prayers... The highest prayer is not one of faith merely; it is demonstration" (Eddy 1906, 10,15-16).

Her healing also illustrates the fact that matter or physical conditions cannot hinder the restorative power of God. Often, such a total opening to the Spirit will transform, not just the illness or handicap, but any bodily abnormality as well, since body embodies or manifests thought. This didn't occur in her case. Marolyn's experience illustrates profoundly that vision is fundamentally mental and spiritual, not dependent on physical eyes.

Her account confirms that we need a spiritual altitude, an unselfed purpose, for God's plan to be fulfilled in us. It's important that we not outline in our thoughts just how or when healing should come, but that we remain faithful and expectant of God's transforming action. For Marolyn, there were many small victories all along the way—victories that equipped her, once she was healed, to encourage and inspire many others.

Scientific Christianity

God's will is always for humanity's healing or salvation. Jesus said plainly: "I came, not to judge the world, but to save the world" (John 12:47); "I am not come to destroy, but to fulfil" (Matt.5:17). Moreover, Jesus' commission to his followers was that they do the works he did, and even greater works—more world-encompassing.

The healing power so clearly evidenced in apostolic Christianity seemed almost lost until it was rediscovered in the 19th Century. Today, it is widely resurgent and practiced, even if not yet fully understood. Its efficacy has been thoroughly attested.

Mary Baker Eddy's prediction concerning the 20th Century: "If the lives of Christian Scientists attest their fidelity to Truth...every Christian church in our land, and a few in far-off lands, will approximate the understanding of Christian Science sufficiently to heal the sick in his name" (Eddy 1895, 22) is rapidly being fulfilled.

She also foresaw (and experienced) the world's resistance to this revitalized and Christianly scientific (provable, verifiable, systematic, thorough) method of healing. After all, her discovery was an intense challenge to the religious and medical beliefs of her day. But the fermentation or change going on since that time in human thinking can't be stopped. The leaven is doing its work.

Christian Science is not, in fact, a church or denomination, though a church was founded to protect and extend its teachings. It is the discovery of the laws or principles underlying Jesus' healing works. Christian Science has brought, not only documented physical healing to many thousands, but has given fresh spiritual insight to a rapidly changing, secularly oriented world. It has produced unmistakable evidence of the fact that God's will or law is done "in earth, as it is in heaven" (Matt.6:10). To those whose lives it has transformed, Christian Science is evidence of the Comforter Jesus foretold, the "Spirit of truth" that would bring to remembrance all that he taught (John 14:16-17,26).

Mrs. Eddy, in an address to her church in 1901, noted this conclusion of the celebrated naturalist, Louis Agassiz: "Every great scientific truth goes through three stages. First, people say it conflicts with the Bible. Next, they say it has been discovered before. Lastly, they say they had always believed it" (Eddy 1901, 27). But she also saw that, for the spiritually committed, popularity has more pitfalls than persecution. Only by taking up the cross—the world's hatred of Truth—and bearing it, she taught, could one win and wear the crown (Eddy, 1906, 254).

She wrote of herself: "The Discoverer of this Science could tell you of timidity, of self-distrust, of friendlessness, toil, agonies, and victories, under which she needed miraculous vision to sustain her..." (Eddy 1891, 17). Again, she urged the members of her church to: "...wait patiently on God; return blessing for cursing; be not overcome of evil, but overcome evil with good; be steadfast, abide and abound in faith, understanding, and good works; study the Bible and the textbook...and follow your Leader only so far as she follows Christ" (Eddy, 1901, 34).

Sadly, throughout human history, religion has too often been used by demagogues, for both personal and political ends. Today, in times that are troubled, uncertain, and changing at great speed, religious fanaticism and extremism are on the rise. Mrs. Eddy, to the contrary, never sought personal eminence or adulation, nor did she make use of political means or seek personal control. Her sole authority was the Bible, though she insisted on its inspired or spiritual meaning. Her entire purpose was the restoration to Christianity of its healing element, and the amelioration of human ills, foremost among them the sinfulness and moral decay that breed disease. Her hope was that others would grasp this practical Science and demonstrate it, thus consistently attaining that direct experience of God or at-one-ment with the Divine that heals.

At this juncture a basic struggle in many areas of society is going on between spiritual values, methods, and practices, and secular materialism. Humanity's progress, like our own, is sometimes slow and always by degrees. At issue fundamentally is the science of being: the underlying laws, knowledge, and truth of being; answers to the unavoidable questions of who, what, and why am I. The extent to which the discoverer of Christian Science and the truths for which she fought have accomplished God's purpose has yet to be fully determined. Her definitive biographer, Robert Peel, feels that "It is as a thinker that Mrs. Eddy will finally be judged." He continues: "...she may well be accounted the metaphysician who pursued spiritual idealism to its furthest extreme and found it, to her own satisfaction, to be solid realism."

"It has been suggested," he writes, "that her unique contribution to world thought was a metaphysic that healed. In the same way it might be said that her unique contribution to Christianity was her concept of the lifework of Jesus Christ as an illustration of demonstrable Science rather than a

miraculous or magical interruption of the natural (i.e. true)
order of things. Only demonstrated facts, she insisted, could
give authority to words that proclaimed...the primacy...of
Spirit" (Peel 1977, 365-366).

She herself states: "What I am remains to be proved
by the good I do" (Eddy 1913, 303). Is that not the ultimate
criterion for us all? In the end, Christianity itself will be
judged solely by the good it has accomplished, and by the
extent to which its healing, redemptive mission has been
fulfilled.

Of this mission, Mrs. Eddy writes: "...Christianity
is not alone a gift, but...a growth Christward; it is not a creed
or dogma...nor the opinions of a sect struggling to gain power
over contending sects... Christianity is the summons of divine
Love for man to be Christlike—to emulate the words and
the works of our great Master. To attain to these works, men
must know somewhat of the divine Principle of Jesus' lifework, and must prove their knowledge by doing as he bade...
The Principle of Christ is divine Love, resistless Life and
Truth. Then the Science (the true knowledge and practice)
of the Principle must be Christlike..." (Eddy 1913, 148-149).

The promise of this Truth or Christ and its unfailing
invitation to humanity remain: "I (Jesus) am the root and
the offspring of David, and the bright and morning star. And
the Spirit and the bride say, Come. And let him that heareth
say, Come. And let him that is athirst come. And whosoever
will, let him take the water of life freely" (Rev.22:16-17).

AUTHORS AND WORKS CITED

Andrew, Brother. 1967. God's smuggler. New Jersey: Fleming H. Revell Co.

Babbitt, Marcy. 1975. Living Christian science. Englewood, New Jersey: Prentice-Hall.

Ballentine, Rudolph. 1990. Decoding the message of illness. Dawn magazine Vol.8, No.1:10-16.

Barnett, Lincoln. 1948. The universe and Dr. Einstein. New York: William Sloane.

Bass, Ellen and Laura Davis. 1988. The courage to heal. New York: Harper and Row.

Beals, Melba Patilla. 1994. Warriors don't cry. New York: Pocket Books.

Benson, Herbert. 1996. Timeless healing: The power and biology of belief. New York: Scribner.

Benson, Mary. 1994. Nelson Mandela: The man and the movement. New York: W.W. Norton and Co.

Blume, E. Sue. 1990. Secret Survivors: Uncovering incest and its after effects in women. New York: Ballantine Books.

Billingsley, K. Lloyd. 1989. The seductive image. Westchester, Illinois: Good News Publishers.

Bradshaw, John. 1988. Bradshaw on: healing the shame that binds you. Deerfield Beach, Florida: Health Communications.

Borysenko, Joan. 1987. Minding the body, mending the mind. Reading, Massachusetts: Addison-Wesley Publishing Co.

————. 1990. Guilt is the teacher, love is the lesson. New York: Warner Books.

Brown, Joanne Carlson and Carole Bohn, editors. 1989. Christianity, patriarchy, and abuse. New York: The Pilgrim Press.

Browning, Don S. 1991. A fundamental practical theology. Minneapolis, Minnesota: Fortress Press.

Carlson, Richard, and Benjamin Shield, editors. 1989. Healers on healing. Los Angeles: Jeremy P. Tarcher, Inc.

Carr, Anne. 1986. On feminist spirituality. In women's spirituality: Resources for Christian development. New York: Paulist Press.

Cashman, Hilary. 1993. Christianity and child sexual abuse. Great Britain: Society for Promoting Christian Knowledge.

Chopra, Deepak. 1990. Perfect health: The complete mind/ body guide. New York: Harmony Books.

Csordas, Thomas J. 1994. The sacred self: A cultural phenomenology of charismatic healing. Berkley: University of California Press.

Cousins, Norman. 1979. Anatomy of an illness. Toronto:Bantam Books.

————. 1984. The healing heart. New York: Avon Books.

Cumminskey, Barbara. 1985. The Miracle Day. Guideposts. April, 1985.

Doehring, Carrie. 1993. Internal desecration: Traumatization and representations of God. Lanham, Maryland: University Press of America.

Dossey, Larry. 1993. Healing words: The power of prayer and the practice of medicine. San Francisco: Harper.

—————. 1996. Prayer is good medicine. San Francisco: Harper.

Droege, Thomas A. 1991. The faith factor in healing. Philadelphia: Trinity Press International.

Drummond, Henry. 1893. The changed life. Westwood, New Jersey: Fleming H. Revell Co.

Eddy, Mary Baker. 1887. Unity of good. Boston: Trustees Under the Will of Mary Baker Eddy.

—————. 1891. No and yes. Boston: Trustees Under the Will of Mary Baker Eddy.

—————. 1891. Retrospection and introspection. Boston: Trustees Under the Will of Mary Baker Eddy.

—————. 1891. Rudimental divine science. Boston: Trustees Under the Will of Mary Baker Eddy.

—————. 1895. Pulpit and press. Boston: Trustees Under the Will of Mary Baker Eddy.

—————. 1896. Christian healing. Boston: Trustees Under the Will of Mary Baker Eddy.

—————. 1896. Miscellaneous writings, 1893-1896. Boston: Trustees Under the Will of Mary Baker Eddy.

——————. 1901. Message for 1901. Boston: Trustees Under the Will of Mary Baker Eddy.

——————. 1906. (First Edition published in 1875). Science and health with key to the Scriptures. Boston: The First Church of Christ, Scientist.

——————. 1913. The First Church of Christ, Scientist and miscellany. Boston: The First Church of Christ, Scientist.

Edwards, Tilden. 1980. Spiritual friend. New York: Paulist Press.

Ford, Marolyn. 1975. These blind eyes now see. Kingsport: Tennessee: Arcata Graphics Co.

Fortune, Marie. 1983. Sexual violence: The unmentionable sin. Cleveland, Ohio: Pilgrim Press.

Forward, Susan and Craig Buck. 1978. Betrayal of innocence. New York: Penguin Books.

Freud, Sigmund. 1995. The basic writings of Sigmund Freud (translated and edited by Dr. A.A. Brill) New York: The Modern Library.

Frankl, Viktor. 1962. Man's search for meaning. Boston: Beacon Press.

Fossum, Merle A. and Marilyn J. Mason. 1986. Facing shame. New York: W. W. Norton and Co.

Framo, J. L. 1984. Family theory and therapy. In Explorations in marital and family therapy. New York: Springer Publishing Co.

Friedman, Edwin H. 1991. Bowen theory and therapy. In Handbook of family therapy, Volume II. New York: Brunner/Mazel.

Gudorf, Christine E. 1992. Victimization: Examining Christian complicity. Philadelphia: Trinity Press.

Harpur, Tom. 1994. The uncommon touch: An investigation of spiritual healing. Toronto: McClelland and Stewart.

Herman, Judith L. 1992. Trauma and recovery. New York: Basic Books.

Hirshberg, Carle and Marc Ian Barasch. 1995. Remarkable recovery: What extraordinary healings tell us about getting well and staying well. New York: Riverhead Books.

Hocking, David. 1990. The moral catastrophe. Eugene, Oregon: Harvest House.

Hunter, Kathryn Montgomery. 1986. 'There was this one guy': The uses of anecdotes in medicine. Perspectives in biology and medicine 29,4 (Summer): 619-630.

Illich, Ivan. 1982. Medical nemesis. New York: Random House.

Imbens, Annie and Ineke Jonker. 1992. Christianity and incest. Minneapolis: Fortress Press.

Inlander, Charles, Lowell Levin and Ed Weiner. 1988. Medicine on trial. New York: Prentice-Hall.

Jordon, Merle. 1986. Taking on the gods. Nashville: Abingdon Press.

Kaufman, Gershen. 1985. Shame: The power of caring.
    Cambridge, Massachusetts: Schenkman Books.

Keller, Ernst and Marie-Luise. 1969. Miracles in dispute: A
    continuing debate. London: SCM Press.

Kelsey, Morton T. 1981. Caring. New York: Paulist Press.

————. 1986. Christianity as psychology. Minneapolis:
    Augsburg Publishing House.

Kubler-Ross, Elizabeth. 1969. On death and dying. New
    York: Macmillan.

Kushner, Harold. 1981. When bad things happen to good
    people. New York: Avon Books.

Kyung, Chung Hyun. 1992. Struggle to be the sun again.
    Maryknoll, New York: Orbis Books.

Leslie, Robert C. 1965. Jesus and logotherapy. New York:
    Abingdon Press.

Lew, Mike. 1988. Victims no longer. New York: Harper and
    Row.

Loftus, Elizabeth and Katherine Ketcham. 1995. The myth
    of repressed memory. Philadelphia: St. Martin's Press.

Madanes, Cloé. 1991. Strategic family therapy. In Handbook
    of family therapy, Volume II. New York: Brunner/
    Mazel.

McCarthy, Barry and Emily. 1993. Confronting the victim
    role. New York: Carroll and Graf Publishers.

McKay, Canon Roy. 1974. Change and the unchanging.
    Guild Lecture No. 177. London: The Guild of
    Pastoral Psychology.

Massie, Robert, Jr. 1982. The constant shadow: Reflections on the life of the chronically ill child. Nashville: Center for the Study of Families and Children, Institute for Public Policy Studies, Vanderbilt University.

Master, Jer. 1980. An interview with Madelon Holland: Why I left the medical profession for Christian Science. Christian Science Journal Vol.98, No.4 (April): 175-178.

—————. 1990. The healing science. Christian Science Sentinel Vol.92, No.25 (18 June): 24-27.

Medved, Michael. 1992. Hollywood versus America. New New York: Harper Collins.

Mendelsohn, Robert. 1979. Confessions of a medical heretic. Chicago: Contemporary Books.

Moyers, Bill. 1993. Healing and the mind. New York: Doubleday.

Muller, Wayne. 1987. Legacy of the heart. New York: Simon and Schuster.

Newgent, Linda and Philip. 1993. Testimony. Christian Science Sentinel Vol.95, No. 51 (20 December): 39-43.

Norton, Nelle. 1985. The journey is home. Boston: Beacon Press.

Nouwen, Henri, 1975. Reaching out. New York: Doubleday.

—————. 1992. Life of the beloved. New York: Crossroad.

Ondrak, John. 1982. Testimony. Christian Science Journal Vol.100, no.9 (September): 543-545.

Payer, Lynn. 1994. Disease mongers. New York: John Wiley.

Peck, M. Scott. 1978. The road less travelled. New York:
    Simon and Schuster.

Peel, Robert. 1977. Mary Baker Eddy: The years of authority.
    (Volume III of a trilogy) New York: Holt, Rinehart and
    Winston.

——————. 1987. Spiritual healing in a scientific age. San
    Francisco: Harper and Row.

Pellauer, Mary D, Barbara Chester and Jane Boyajian,
    editors. 1987. Sexual assault and abuse. New York:
    Harper and Row.

Person, Ethel. 1980. Sexuality as the mainstay of identity:
    psychoanalytic perspectives. Signs 5: 605-630.

Peterson, Ralph E. 1982. A study of the healing church and
    its ministry. New York: Lutheran Church in America.

Powell, Margaret. 1986. Profile: Forgiveness in Beirut.
    Christian Science Sentinel Vol.88, No.3 (20 January):
    102-107.

Poyser, Margaret. 1995. Why Christian Science is practical
    in healing children. Christian Science Sentinel Vol.97,
    No.10 (6 march): 3-7.

Redfern, J.W.T. 1975. Can we change? (Lecture No. 179)
    London: Guild of Pastoral Psychology.

Russell, Diana E.H. 1986. The secret trauma: Incest in the
    lives of girls and women. New York: Basic Books.

Richardson, Jamae Wolfram. 1987. My grace is sufficient
    for thee. Christian Science Journal Vol.105, No.4
    (April): 5-7.

————————. 1994. Omnipresence. Christian Science Journal Vol.112, No.7 (July): 33-34.

Sanford, Agnes. 1947. The healing light. St.Paul, Minnesota: Macalester Park Publishing Co.

————————. 1966. The healing gifts of the Spirit. New York: Harper and Row.

Shengold, Leonard. 1989. Soul murder. New York: Ballantine Books.

Siegel, Bernie. 1986. Love, medicine, and miracles. New York: Harper and Row.

————————.1989. Peace, love, and healing. New York: Harper and Row.

Smyth, Myrtle. 1993. The time for forgiveness has arrived. Christian Science Journal Vol.111, No.12 (December): 15-17.

Stendahl, Krister. 1991. Conversations. Christian Science Sentinel Vol.93, No.18 (6 May): 3-7.

Stockdale, Jim and Sybil. 1984. In love and war. New York: Harper and Row.

Ten Boom, Corrie. 1983. The hiding place. New York: Bantam Books.

Tillich, Paul. 1957. The meaning of faith. Chicago: Exploration Press.

van Eck, Bart. 1989. Testimony. Christian Science Journal Vol.107. No.6 (June): 37-38.

Whitehead, Barbara Defoe. 1993. Dan Quayle was right. Atlantic Monthly Vol.271, No.4 (April): 47-84.

Wilson, Gordon. 1988. Marie: A story from Enniskillen. An Interview. Christian Science Sentinel Vol.94, No.42 (17 October): 19-22.

Wimber, John. 1987. Power healing. San Francisco: Harper and Row.

Wink, Walter, 1994. The other world is here. Christian Century (27 April): 443.

Wyndham, John H. 1994. The ultimate freedom. Long Beach, California: Mountaintop Publishing.

INDEX

ABOUT THE AUTHOR

Jamae van Eck is a practitioner of spiritual healing with 30 years of experience. She has been listed in the Christian Science Journal since 1967. She has relied on the efficacy of the spiritual method she advocates for a lifetime, as did her mother and grandmother. She became an authorized teacher of Christian Science in 1979 and has been published frequently in the Christian Science periodicals.

She graduated from Wellesley College in 1953 and completed a Master's Degree in Theological Studies at Boston University's School of Theology in 1995. She taught school, served in both Michigan and Ohio as a College Organization Advisor and as a speaker for the Christian Science Committee on Publication, and has been active in many capacities, including that of First Reader, in branch churches of Christ, Scientist in various locations.

Currently she is serving on the Boards of the Arden Wood Sanatorium in San Francisco and the Clairbourn School in San Gabriel. She has three grown children and two grandchildren and lives in suburban Los Angeles.

ACKNOWLEDGEMENTS

My special thanks go to the following:

Certain faculty and staff at the Boston University School of Theology, especially my academic advisor, for the compassion, openness, and support they have expressed;

Lynne Bundesen, my editor, for her generous, effective, and always constructive assistance, and for her enthusiastic encouragement;

All those who were willing to share their own stories—over and above already published accounts—in the hopes their experiences could be of help to others (in some cases names have been changed for individuals' protection);

Friends whose reading of the initial manuscript and suggestions as it evolved helped immeasurably to clarify and strengthen its message;

My husband, Bart van Eck, for his careful reading and re-reading of the book, his alert and always thoughtful comments, and for his unfailing wise counsel in this effort.

WHAT READERS ARE SAYING...

"This is a wonderfully integrative work, insightful and compassionate, that grounds healing in the life of the Spirit and recalls us again and again to that truth."
> Dr. Theresa Sherf
> Pastor, Union Church, Berea Kentucky
> Former Religion Professor, Berea College

"This well-written book seeks a wider recognition of the practice of spiritual healing based on the Bible. Jamae van Eck provides many useful examples of spiritual conquest over all kinds of human maladies. She writes for everyone seeking a higher sense of individual freedom."
> Dr. Frank Darling
> Author and speaker on Biblical healing
> Ruskin, Florida

"This courageous book is a must-read for the steadfast solution seekers of today. It offers a uniquely researched and spiritually-based healing balm for the cruel and often unjustly inflicted wounds to individual worth and dignity."
> Betty Jo Hunt, nursing consultant
> Former Superintendent of Nurses at Tenacre Foundation, Princeton, New Jersey; Supervisor of patients with mental and emotional challenges

"To the question 'Wilt thou be made whole?' comes the eager answer: Yes. Yes. Yes. This book points the way."
> P. Arnsen Blakely, Partner in the law firm of Davis, Samuelson, Blakely & Goldberg, LLP
> Costa Mesa, California

"To read this book is to be drawn into the experience of healing, especially with regard to the discovery of who we are and have been. The author's words come out of a center focused on a life with God."
> Dr. John W. Ward, Ordained Methodist Minister and Pastor, Cuttyhunk Island Union Church; Retired Associate Professor of Communication and Preaching, Boston University School of Theology

ORDER FORM

<u>Telephone orders and inquiries</u>: Call Toll Free: 1 (800) 417-5220

<u>FAX orders</u>: 1 (800) 417-5220

<u>On-line orders</u>: Panthaleon @AOL.COM

Mail orders: Panthaleon Press
P.O. Box 70669
Pasadena, California 91117-7669

Price: $14.95 (In Canada $19.95)
Twenty per cent discount for orders of ten or more

Sales tax: Please add 8.25% for books shipped to California addresses

Shipping and handling costs:
Book rate: $2.50 for the first book and $1.00 for each additional copy to the same address
(Surface mail may take three to four weeks)

First Class: $3.00 per book

Priority Mail: $4.00 per book

Payment: ❏ cheque

❏ credit card: Visa ❏   Master Card ❏

Card Number: _____

Expiration Date:_____

Name on card:_____

Please send_____copies to:

Name_____

Address_____

City_____ State _____ Zip_____

Telephone (_____)_____

Panthaleon Press will send your gift copies directly to other recipients at your request. Please attach a separate sheet of addressees.

Any copies may be returned for a full refund within thirty days of purchase.